The
Compl
NothingDoings

**in which is elaborated
a wondrous liberation
epistemopoetology
(of sorts)**

Amir Parsa

The

Complete

NothingDoings

in which is elaborated
a wondrous liberation
epistemopoetology
(of sorts)

Amir Parsa

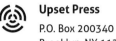

Upset Press
P.O. Box 200340
Brooklyn, NY 11220
upsetpress.org

The Complete NothingDoings
Published in New York by UpSet Press
Copyright © 2019 by Amir Parsa

Established in 2000, UpSet Press is an independent press based in Brooklyn. The original impetus of the press was to upset the status quo through literature. UpSet Press has expanded its mission to promote new work by new authors; the first works, or complete works, of established authors—placing a special emphasis on restoring to print new editions of exceptional texts; and first-time translations of works into English. Overall, UpSet Press endeavors to advance authors' innovative visions, and works that engender new directions in literature.

Library of Congress Control Number: 2019944703
ISBN 978-1-937357-82-5
First printing: Fall 2019

Book design by Wendy Lee / wendyleedesign.com

*A big thank you to
my daughter Oriana,
in whose presence
the first drafts
of most of these texts
were written
(with pen on paper).*

A. And in the Perdurable

Spirit of a Breviloquent

Manifesto...

The NothingDoings of Amir Parsa constitute a radical shift away from the *production of objects* AND from the *curation of non-object-centered experiences*, a general poetics that leads to—without ever claiming adherence to—the 'art-ing' of the living of life. I should, perhaps, reword that: the NoDos (pronounced 'NoDoh' and not 'NoDoo') *also* disrupt the art/life paradigm that is a bit 'in vogue' as of this writing, the 'life-as-form' paradigm, the 'ephemeral aesthetic' paradigm, the 'relational art' paradigm—you get my drift. Not only do the NoDos constitute a *new way of creating* art and a *new art form*—and in the process shift the paradigm of artistic creation and the epistemological, aesthetic and social *quiddity* of art—but they also, through the subtle operations at work in each *type* of NoDo, shift the paradigm of *living* and of *experiencing art*, and even shift the *paradigm of paradigm-shifting*.

That's right: it can be put forth with much aplomb that the NothingDoings, in their variety, their irreverence, their humor *and* their rigor, had *and* have, as core principal objectives: to save art from itself, save the artists from excessive drowning in the mechanisms of the art world, save a downward spiral into the perpetual construction of objects and the production of non-objects, and lead to or at least propose a rebellion against these modes of fashioning art. The NothingDoings invite, I should say *impose*, a pause, a reconsideration, a radical shift as I alluded to above, a *shift of shifting,* towards, well, justement, the NoDo. A well-needed, crucial *pause*, I say again, a necessary *cessation of activities* in the regular realm, a cessation of *excessive activitation* (that's right activi*t*ation—not a typo) in the regular regime, in favor of *non-activities*, or, more accurately, *a-activities*, ultimately making the phenomenological processes that allow the arts to be part of our lives—that is, *seeing*, *feeling*, *breathing* etc.—the constitutive components of the artworks themselves.

·

One is tempted to dub the adventure *The Degree Zero of Art*, or *Art Degree Zero*, a tabula rasa of aesthetic consideration and artistic practice. Were it not for the fact that Parsa himself did conceive *The Degree Zero of Art* (DeZA)—where he pointedly included three of his works: the book of *The Complete Nothing-Doings*, the hilarious *Loafapalooza* (itself made of a sub-trilogy, namely *Éloge du Brouillon*, *La Gloria del Quit*, and *In Praise of Idleness*), and the sublimely witty and delirious *Conceptual Conceptualism*—we would be well-situated to introduce the term and implant it as the foundation of a reconsideration of where art begins, how art is formulated, and how art is propounded and disseminated. In fact, any one of these works could easily have stood for the DeZA by itself, but it is a tribute to Parsa for having conceived—and having the guts to actually present—such works as artworks, risking his own skin, as it were, to, as I like to say, *stop the madness of perpetual production or even announced non-production*! He knowingly undertakes an adventure that is dangerous for his career, let alone for a work that surely could go on and get mocked. And he knowingly—and this is perhaps something his harsher critics do not quite grasp—in our current atmosphere, humbly accepts becoming the rebel child against all faux rebels. We salute him, then, and we shall cease this introduction, and let the work *thrust* its own truthness upon our souls!

•

Well, not quite yet, sorry! First, a few more elaborations—and, again, apologies for not turning to the

NoDos just yet. The reader will note, soon enough, that the *texts of the NoDos* here rédigés are infused with purposely ambiguous, often paradoxical drivel, at times inching close to absurdist levels. This we have noted even: linguistically perplexing unfoldings shed light on the absurdity and the strangeness of the functioning of the art world, while simultaneously contributing poignant theory and critiques—a subtle line between humorous and unsettling that is beautifully explored in the NoDos.

One wonders though, and correctly you would assume, why there are any NoDos in the first place, why they exist that is, and how they came to be—a consideration that is inevitably contemporaneous with the question of the very *quiddity* (the *whatness*) of the No-Dos. Not hard to figure out, really. For one, we could point to the excessive amount of productions, of creations, of works experienced: of works that are *manifest*. There are just too many. And by writing 'too many' we are not ascribing value: it's not that there is 'lots of crap out there' like many like to say (even though that also is true)—there is in fact an abundance of quality work. Truth is, there are simply *too many* works, *too much* production, *too many* objects, *too many* experiences, simply put, *too much*, and certainly, *enough*! More works that are *manifest* are not needed! Second, although we acknowledge that the quiddity of works has indeed come under much scrutiny by many, and that there are quite a few works that are not only ephemeral, not only in the *lignée* of life/artworks, but some that are not even manifest in palpable ways, we still argue that even those that are not manifest are *announced*. And thus, again, *too much* stuff! The power, beauty, position, and aesthetics of the NothingDoings lie in their lack of being *manifest AND* their lack of being *announced.* That is the key, and that is the thing. Or should I be writing: that is the thing, and it is key.

One consideration that is brought to our attention (in those few secret conversations that we have had regarding the nature and future of the NothingDoings) is the work of the 'artists without works' or *artistes sans œuvre* (ASO). We have heard the argument that among the champions of the non-manifest and non-announced, we have these radical *artistes sans œuvre*, or those who espouse the art/life paradigm, with theoretical acumen and with deep and profound knowledge of art history and theory and the legacy of artistic forms. Surely, we respond, that is to say, yes indeed, the NoDos are *aligned* with that legacy, are *sympathetic* brethren, but again, we insist: the art/life artists, those whose works may have no objecthood, whose works have successfully overcome the need for the construction or production of objects, even those who have overcome the fashioning of experiences without objects, whether ephemeral or not, those who have convincingly argued for and exposed life-as-form artworks that go beyond the creation of objects and experiences outside of life-as-form, even they often have made *manifest* their quote unquote works. And... Even if it could be argued that they have not made them manifest any differently than simply *living*, they still make them *announced*, in any number of venues and through any number of ways, that being the only way for the life-as-form artists to actually make the argument for their art.

In the case of the *artistes sans œuvre* more specifically, whether they create works that are not objects but *manifest*, or they make no outwardly works but *announce* their lives or some other non-work as art, we can see the similarities but clearly note the difference with the essence of the NothingDoings. In a third potential case, if the ASO's contribution could be said to be *without manifestation* and *unannounced*—although we would argue that the very announcement of an artist without an œuvre IS the announcement of the artwork—even in this case, even if we were to grant lack of manifestation and lack of announcement, the ASO's position (and the attendant mythology) resides in *œuvrelessness*! Thus, the ultimate differentiation: the NothingDoings *do constitute an artwork*, a *type of artwork*, and thus their progenitor is certainly not arguing for being an artist without an œuvre, but *with* an œuvre, creating a *type of artwork* indeed, an umbrella term that has many subtypes under *a NothingDoing*! And we insist—and the reader must closely pay attention to and consider the *a*—it is *a NothingDoing* that thrives on being *not manifest* and *unannounced*. Thus, Parsa would argue that the closest thing to the NothingDoings probably being the non-work of the *artistes sans œuvre*—the closest brethren of the NoDoist, in effect—the differentiation is clear: the ASOs either create works that are any combination of manifest and announced while claiming to have no œuvre, or they are tending towards living a life where the works are unmanifest and unannounced, but again, remain without an œuvre. Parsa repeats constantly that the NothingDoings constitute *an art form*! Their progenitor is not claiming to be an artist without an œuvre, despite appearances and despite the lack of object-creation, experience-creation, or any other manifestation. The NothingDoings are made up of various *types* of works, each of which may have subtle variations and iterations (a *subtype*), each of which in turn can be spun into another *sub-subtype* of NothingDoing, each with its own *title*, each in turn always questioning the art form and constantly rejuvenating the interrogations around and the positions at the foundations of the art form—alive, evolutive, transforming, and dare I say, fabulous.

We have thus touched on some important and necessary aspects of the NoDos, and also add the following, which shall correctly be deemed obvious by the artistically literate: the NoDos constitute a *critique in action*, a critique *en route*, an *ur-critique*, a protest, a cry, and, again, *a construction of a resistance movement against,* and *critique of*, sensory overload, excess of visual images, excessive number of announcements, excessive number of manifest artworks and objects, excessive art world machinations, excessive ambitions and desires. A necessary evolution of the critique of the art world's and artworks' separation from political arenas, and, obviously, a continuing critique of the institutions and the rituals of these worlds.

A real *artwork* then—within the legacy of critique, and with *kinship* with relational works, performance, ephemeral and conceptual artworks, institutional critique works; a champion of disruption, of paradigm shifting; sympathetic to previous movements but distancing itself through its *non-manifestation and its unannouncement*. And *a piece of prose* that serves as the lone document, but also as part of the artwork, in that, as will be noted, the *telling* is *part* of the work—this telling, the only telling.

·

Lastly, but perhaps firstly, and this time I promise to cede way to the various NothingDoings right after, the query I wish to bring forth is the following: is this document, after all, not an *excuse* for the *elaboration* of a different, deviously unexpected and pioneering *literary genre*? In other words, its progenitor known to be a truly vanguardish *literary* innovator, is this not simply the touch of ingenuity whereby a whole other edifice is built, rituals designed and fomented, a wondrous universe of methods of writing/thinking/circulating elaborated, under the guise of art, within a whole other universe of discourse, with the devilishly clever intention of fashioning a new way of writing, truly a new *genre*, I say again, which is founded on the new *form* that is at play at the discursive level? The only way in which it could be conceived and rendered is under the guise of *a document of an artwork* that is, in fact, in a hidden and secret manner, a slim yet innovative piece of prose, constructing a dazzlingly simple yet unnerving relationship with reality, using a variety of modalities of scription, slightly yet significantly manipulating and juxtaposing them in such ways that philosophical conundrums, humorous phraseology, serious arguments etc. are simultaneously present to describe an artwork and its iterations. A *literary* master stroke, after all, this *scription of the NothingDoing*, documenting supposedly the tale of the fashioning of a masterful *artwork*, the actual creation of the NothingDoings, the making, performance, or rather *a-making, a-performance* of a NothingDoing. Where the *simultaneous operation and conception* lead to two, count them, *two, major, paradigm, shifts! In both art AND literature*!! Is this not, after all, that effort, and that realization! Is it not... Query, again, without the mark to dub it so. That indeed is where one has tread. That is perhaps the unconscious inspiration, the true calling of the progenitor of the whole shebang. Yes, perhaps... But perhaps not, as well... What is known, is that we have on our hand a *literary gem,* a piece that is also a *document* that reveals a wondrous, original, liberating *type* of *art form*, *the NothingDoing*. Yes, wondrous adventures, an arting of life that is a critique of art that is, in the guise of a document, a literary diamond in the rough. All that, yes, and why not... Now, as promised, I shall give way to the NothingDoings themselves, as elaborated and practiced, and subsequently written, by their author...

— Amir Parsa

B. Prolegomena to the Theory/Praxis of a Revolutionary Emancipatory Art Form

(From Prologue for the Anagraphika to The Triumph of the NothingDoings)

1. Prologue for the Anagraphika

The epiphany came to me when I, floating on the blue waters of the Caribbean, looked up in the sky and saw the tips of the palm trees, and saw the blue of the sky, and saw the tops of the roofs and saw in the sky the whiteness of the clouds, and saw beyond the sky—I say, *I saw beyond the sky*...

It happened when I turned my head back down and in my eternal gaze, in my piercing gaze, I turned and saw around me the heads in the sea, the bodies in the sea, the bodies walking on the sand, the rhythm of the bodies, the paces of the gaits, the faces and the waves that I heard...

And then how I looked upwards again: how I looked *upwards* I say, in such manner that no one before me had ever gazed upwards I'm convinced, and saw the branches and the cables and the rooftops and the streaks of clouds in the blue. This is where it happened. It was to be called Composition Number One, and yes, the epiphany of CNO would change forever the course of art history, of photographic history, of image-making history, of trace-making history—understand me, benevolent reader: that means, the history of art, the history of literature, the history of graph-making indeed!

Revolutionary, I must say, for was it not, it was, it was, I insist, it was the purest form of photography: the instant captured, the image in its purest form, the *graphy* of light! How can one imagine that a photograph would be so pure—and forever captured, and, here is the epiphany, forever ungraphed! *Forever ungraphed*, that was the revolution: there would be, there will be, no more objects with traces—but a world of artworks, *without traces*! The purest form of art it was: the *story of mark-ing itself*, through the refusal to mark that very moment. Literature in its purest form: words unuttered, poems unwritten, texts unfashioned! Tracelessness across art forms! *Tracelessness across disciplines*!

•

This is not a manifesto! Let me repeat: this is not a manifesto—because all works will henceforth have, in their body, a theory of the practice embedded. No more manifestoes then, or... Ah, let me stop, at once! And say this: I offered to put this in a document, or else, as all friends insisted, how can we know of the works without traces?! How will anyone know of the works without traces?! That's just it, I agreed, some-how reluctantly, that is it: I too must also succumb to the great tyranny—and leave a *document*!

Many arguments were made, many points debated! It will be thought of as *conceptual*, they said! Argh, I shuddered. Argh, I repeated! Not conceptual, not con-ceptual, I kept yelling! They'll just say it was *perfor-mance*, others uttered! No, I cried! No no no, not mere-ly performative! A work, an artwork, a new type, a new way, I insist, a new world! A joke, still others insisted. If you don't leave at least one document, one note, that says what it's all about, how it came to be, how it goes on, they'll say it was nonsense, or a ruse, or, worse, a joke—if they even know what *it* was! 'And besides,' an-other obviously lucid friend throws out, 'the best you'll get is that you started an oral tradition, a different *kind* of oral tradition, a myth, the smarter cats might even say, a legend, and the rest, forget it, they won't get it at all. An intriguing idea in and of itself,' he went on, 'but not exactly what you want, and what you're doing.' Righto righto, the words under my tongue, my head in its wobbling approving, not what I am saying after all, not what I'm doing! No, not quite, not at all, in fact, a new type, I murmured, a new world, I insist! 'It's not so much that this is a new type of, well, artwork, or an intervention of sorts,' this same friend murmurs shyly, 'it's that, it's a challenge to the paradigm of creative work, and a challenge to the modes of critique and intervention we're used to, right? Critique of the definitions of art, of life, of being, of living—I think that's what it is, right?' He stops suddenly, pauses, waitingly...

O how right he was, O how right he is, O how right you are, I wanting to blurt out, I wanting to shout out, such clairvoyance, such lucidity, such thoughtfulness and glorious and envious clarity! How could I refute these fabulous points! How could I begin to even remotely think that I might not do it! A note then, I shuddered, a note, I will write: for all those who ever think of abandoning, of not doing, of not participating, all those who'd like to reject the trace, and yet move on living and fashioning works of art, without traces, for all those who sit and contemplate, we need the catalogue of the exhibition of the works, a catalogue, lo a *catalogue raisonné* why not (not!), of the wondrous *works without traces: the Anagraphika, the works without traces!*

·

Anagraphika: the tire and the cross, burning in the middle of a street in Santo Domingo... And the image is fixed, and the work is seen, and the works that I shall produce with it, also fixed: no need, then, to make the object. And almost immediately, the image is transformed. I tell my companion, that is Anagraphika number such and such—and sure, I invent the numbers, for I have no idea how many there have been (just another among the many I have successfully fashioned). And thus the telling becomes part of the work: for I tell the story of the Anagraphika, of the works without traces, and the telling becomes part of the story, part of the work. And then we move on, marvel on, carry on.

This was not a particular work within a medium, but the extension of a major problematic, the insistence on confronting a problematic of the field, the field of all that has come to pass as *art*, my friends. Consider that moment: the moment of an act, a breath, a vision, an image, in all its glory; then, simply with your own perception, your own being, you capt it, record it. Even without a machine, without an actual tool and without the subsequent trace, that act can be deemed photographic: it is the beginning of the photographic—the writing of light, through our vision and through the viewing and through the forming. Here though, immediately afterwards, the image is transformed, and in perpetual state of transformation it carries on, moving on and becoming other than what it is/was: the instant into eternity. The instant forever captured and replayed and relayed, and becoming elsewhat in its tracelessness: the eternally transforming image has become an artwork, a different type of photograph, a traceless artwork. An ephemeral capturing. Efemerata, yes, works of ephemeral quality, that I very specifically refuse to capture through any tool, or machine, or mechanism, and that actually captures the ephemeral essence in the purest manner. An *ongoing ephemeral artwork*. The glory of the Anagraphika is that the ephemeral remains so, and transforms into an eternal ephemeral work, through the image, through the transformation, through the telling.

An ephemeral account too. The telling itself transformed in turn. Ephemeral ephemerality. Beyond, there is no sign, there is no word, there is no material—and no trace! No one knows about the thousands of works that I have produced—and that is just as well! I tell of the works, I tell the neighbors, I tell the friends, I tell those who accompany me, those around me, those whose lives touch mine: the artworks I have fashioned, circulated in the telling among the disciples and the friends. Limited numbers, and limited numbers of people who know of them, but O how glorious! We have redefined materiality itself—beyond the material, beyond the immaterial, into ur-material: Anagraphika! Can you feel the impact!

I have liberated all from all traces: a long goodbye, and a smashing of the idols. But you should know that all those claiming to be smashers of idols, they were among those who knew the idols well—too well, all too well! The works without traces, before the beginning as if unborn: to be born into a new world, to be born again, into the new world, and inviting all to inherit the wondrousness, the glory, of the new consciousness.

•

I had made the mistake of calling them Efemerata, I explained to friends! Friends, I cried, I have seen the light (literally)! Friends, I have found the solution! Friends, I have overcome the movements and the isms and the fetishes of our time! I told them: I will tell you the story of my Efemerata! And I told them: the epiphany came to me when I was floating on the blue water of the Caribbean Sea: how I looked upwards and saw the rooftops and the skyclouds and the treebranches and the lightgraphs—and how I knew never to give trace anymore, to my creations! But then I realized soon enough that the Efemerata needed to be renamed, for they carried still the stigma of the trace, ephemeral as it may have been, the name carried the *proposal* of the trace. But a new freedom was on the way, for the foundations of tracelessness were being implanted. A glorious future awaited us, O Anagraphika!

Ah then, friend, they said, this is very much a conceptual construct you speak of! No, no I insisted, it is not a conceptual construct, it is an *actual work*, it's just that it bears *no trace*—I repeat, not a mere conceptual construct! It is a mental image then, a pure abstraction, they hollered! I like the idea, I muttered, but no, not a pure abstraction either: it is a *work*, liberated from the tenets of objecthood! How then do we know of it, they said. And I told them how the Efemerata were now the works without traces, and that the story of their coming into being, the telling, was part of the work, inevitably. Ah, but you have made the story into the art, came their retort, isn't storytelling an art to begin with?! But no, no, friends ('no, friends' rapidly turning into 'nofriends' as I became ever more agitated), I insisted, I have not, what the hell is wrong with you! The telling is part of the work: it is not performance, it is not storytelling, it is not a conceptual piece. It unfolds, a work, without a trace, works without traces, and the telling the one remnant. I have done the works, and the question is: how does one become aware of the works without traces?! And I said, I shall tell you of it: and the story of the telling, becomes a part of the work: that is the story of the works without traces. This smacks of philosophy, they charged! You are philosophizing, they charged—unaware of my contentious relationship with philosophers of all kinds. What use is this sort of philosophizing again when so many before you have done so, philosophers and not! What use is it?! They kept hammering away and repeating, 'What use is it?!'

It is of no use, I countered, how right you are, how I agree with you, it is of no use at all!! It is conceptual art, others countered again and endlessly, and I, 'No, no it's not!' It is, they insisted, it IS, don't deny it you jackass, it's neo neo-conceptual! And I, 'No, I insist, it's not, and I'm not a jackass and in fact, y'all are the jackasses!' And so many before you have done conceptual art, they insisted, you're full of shit and this is BS! What do you mean BS, one of my friends intervened in this particular episode that I recognize is quickly turning into a narrative of one instance of vehement refutation and seems to be leaning toward some sort of coming-to-blows or street fight or something, but which it really didn't even come close to. Ahhh I shuddered, arghhh, I whimpered, I just keep telling you it's NOT conceptual art you morons, holding back the protective friend—it is not conceptual art! I said: I am not much for 'conceptual' art, hear me! Or what is dubbed conceptual art! There is *concept* in every art form, there are *conceptual machinations* in every innovative artistic gesture and production! All damn art, or all damn good art, has a new conceptual component! The concept is always present! There are always conceptual operations at work in an innovative concoction! One is aware of them or not. One uses and manipulates them or not. One does such things that bring operations upon material or not. No, not conceptual art! Conceptual, no, I repeated, conceptual, no! *Obras sin huellas*. *Obras sin rastros*, that's what it's all about! It's not just the idea here mattering, it is also the execution, a particular skill it takes to leave works without traces! Hear me, understand me (this now I was not telling to that particular group, but to all), try to come with me on this adventure: there is a particular learned skill to fashion and continue the creation of works without traces! This is a major contribution to the history of art, of photography, of image-making, of mark-making! For, what is every object, every artistic object, in and of itself: it is, first and foremost, a *trace*—and I'm ushering in the era of *works without traces*!

•

I made the mistake of calling them Efemerata, I say again! That assumed that they were ephemeral: that they existed in concrete form, and that they vanished, shed their concrete objectness. I made a mistake and I am here admitting it. In fact, even the conceptualists and the neo-conceptualists and their heroes and superheroes, they too fell into the *object* trap. They made the objects, they lived with the objects. But I, my friends, from the get-go, I was able to escape it! There are no objects here, these are works without traces—and I stand here and tell you of them. And you laugh, and you smile: and that, in and of itself, IS, the telling of the being of the Anagraphika. For these are not ephemeral works, nor has their quiddity been transformed: they have always been works without traces, always without form; or shall I say that within their formlessness, they are constantly being transformed. Yes, my brethren, read this expression again and bask in the glory that it brings: in formlessness, they are constantly, and eternally, transformed. Who would dare propose that they have come up with higher, bolder, more fabulous, works of art? Not Efemerata, but Anagraphika!

Soon—and before we know it—the theorists and historians will make a *typology*, lo, a *taxonomy*, of *works without traces*. There will be museums dedicated to works without traces. Exhibitions and celebrations and presentations and festivities. All around *works without traces*. And let me announce this now, my brethren, the festivities will be more breathtaking, more fire-and-lightning, more thunderous and more fabulously phantasmagoric than all the festivities you have up to now heard of! There will be the Day of the New Era, the Day of the First Rising, and a new world will be ushered in: a whole new unbrave world, a world of absences and passages, a world of dust and fragments, a world of whispers and sudden dashes, a world of scurrying and a world of secrets! All around the city will be adorned with the works without traces! All around, the colors and the lines of the works without traces will be the new design! All around, the piercing gazes back at the works without traces will be thrust upon the motions and the stillnesses of the world! All around, the world of worlds without traces!!

·

Have you, like me, seen the struggles of all the artists seeking exhibitions?! All challenging and desiring and wanting and clamoring: to *show*! What a word indeed: to *show*! What exercises in vanity—although you can correctly claim that all, all of it, all of this, all of all art making and lit writing, all is vanity! But then again, the show! How many in their silent voices could have clamored: save me, save us, from the weight, from the pressure, from the needs we feel, to *show*! And that prophet would have been false who would only have comforted them in their non-showing, in their non-participation, lo, in their non-exhibition—because they wanted it! How heavy-handed the exhibitions and the non-exhibitions! The Anagraphika, at first, and the NothingDoings subsequently, have successfully paved the way and cleared the path for the *unexhibitable*! That, my friends, is where paradise lies, that is where there is hope and freedom and that is where the sanctuary lies! All should bow down and hold me aloft after their prayer for fashioning such a sanctuary: for it was impossible to have an exhibition of the Anagraphika in the early days of our formulation of these fabulous ventures, being as they were, traceless, integrating in the very fabric of their eternal unfolding, the telling of the story of all the previous manifestations and non-manifestations of the Anagraphika!

How dare they propose an exhibition for the Anagraphika, I screamed in those early days! Believe me, I have even tried! During a 'solo' exhibition, I had a man standing in the middle of this mostly empty gallery telling the story of the transforming unfoldings that constitute the grand organon that is the Anagraphika! Images and material entities that suddenly morph into material immaterialities, and in turn into tales, told, unfolding along with their brethren. And if such a man were to continue to stand in the middle of a gallery or a museum or a street even, and call his work and his presence the best approximation of an exhibition of the Anagraphika, they would be quick to say performance art; or better yet, conceptual and performance art! No, let us live at peace with this! We have liberated you all from the exhibition and the non-exhibition, dug the grave of the *exhibitory practice*—dug its grave! Carry along, happily! Giddily, giddily carry along, comfortable in the glorious unfolding, the eternal unfolding organon that the Anagraphika first launched and that the NothingDoings continue to fashion!

How then to give an account of the Anagraphika?! How, yes, how?! Those who came before made the great mistake of capturing, through prisms and objects, their ephemeral constructions. And not only the masses, but the connoisseurs, the curators, the other artists, went for it! No my friends, I plead with you to think about this: what is the account of the ephemeral, the account of the Anagraphika, the account of the NothingDoing? How must one action it, bring it into being? And as I partly thought that even these questions were wrong, I was persuaded, perhaps by my own instincts, to make the one document, the one manifestation of the overall shebang...

I began to tell the story: the story of the becoming of the works. I told of how the story that the telling launches is part of the work. It is not the telling of the story. It is the telling that launches the story. I wonder if the populace feels, fathoms, understands, I should say, the force of what I have written here: it is the telling that launches the tale. That *makes* the tale. An example: I'm walking with a colleague when she encounters a piece of torn paper on the floor of a most eminent museum, right after we have gone through an exhibition that tells the story of lines, grids, and stains, and where the very last 'piece' we had witnessed was a paper torn in pieces assembled and exhibited. I say to her, there, that is part of the Anagraphika. What is? says she. I say, *that*, your picking up this piece of paper. It is a *photograph of a performative* event. It is performance and photography. Suddenly, the paper falls as she picks it up. There again, says I, *that* is number two, you picking up the torn piece of paper from the museum floor! She says, 'That's kind of cool!' Indeed, says I, more than cool, it is coolissimo! 'And kind of corny,' she laughs. Cornissimo, laugheth I—and that is the point! And this, our exchange, our laughter, our smiles, our comments, our words that we invented, these too, are part of the work, concludeth I as we walk down the hallway.

Part of the work. The telling launches a story that in turn leads to more telling—the telling that the story launches—for again, I had only begun to tell her the story of the Anagraphika that a telling was launched, and the telling fashioned new worlds, and the telling fashioned new stories, and the telling fashioned new events, and the telling fashioned a new me, and a new her, and a new world, and a new reality. Can the populace truly understand the breadth of what I am suggesting? Of the revolution that is steeped deep within this momentous illustration: the making of new worlds, the making of new realities, all from the telling of the story of the Anagraphika—of the works without traces!

Have I not thus ushered in a new meaning of life!? Laugh not those of you who are tempted: those who, for example, are taking this exposition as the ramblings of a madman, or of a fraudulent fornicator—and you know who you are; or those who immediately think of the very funny, I admit, 'meaning-of-life' comedy movies, or other comics or books that told us of the impossibility of even attempting such forays. See my friend's bending to pick up the paper: it was imbued with life-force upon the hearing of the telling. My laughter and the words that came from her: imbued with life, with motion, with depth, with passion, with the *souffle*, says I, the breath, the fire, of life! Each of the steps that we took, each of the atomic, sub-atomic trillion operations our neurological systems went through for each action and reaction and more in that millisecond, each was imbued with meaning, with joy, with reason for being. I am convinced, yes, that the erasure of the necessity of the object, the rupture with the centuries, lo millennia, of the fetish of objects, and, in addition, the overcoming of the production of experiences as a substitute for the creation of the objects, that is, then, the *double overcoming*, has ushered in, through the Anagraphika, and the varieties of NothingDoings, a powerful, immovable, unavoidable surge into liberty! The one freedom that is disallowed—beyond our consciousness, indeed.

What is *this* then?! What is *this* book?! What is this booklet?! Is this a book?! What is a book?! This book, you might ask, what is this book?! Is it not a trace?!!! Angrily perhaps you are reading and saying, is this not a trace, you *farceur*, not a *trace*, this, an *object* even, you fraud?!! It is not I say, no, it is not, it is NOT and I must answer that it is not! It is the trace of tracelessness. But it is the only one. The one I shall permit myself. The only one! A document for tracelessness! The one document of tracelessness! Not just another in the full spectrum of conceptual concoctions? Not another in the tired amalgam of weightless fabrications? Ah, how I peer patiently at such charges, and think again, no, this book is a mere document, a paean to the Anagraphika, to the NothingDoings too as we shall soon see, the one document for all the works. There is no video, no photograph, no other form of documentation. This is it. The one documentation. It.

•

But what is a trace, O prophet of tracelessness! Have you told us the tale of traces, if so proudly you sing the praise of tracelessness! Have you even begun to define the notion of trace, the notion of doing, the notion of nothing, and how they have developed, and their historical manifestations, and their theoretical mutations, and how different folks have conceived of them, before you can launch this precious and pre-scient attack on tracefulness, and manifestation, and announcements, O prophet of tracelessness?! Have you given an account of all the beauty that has been brought to the world, the meaning that has been given to places and spaces and people through the work of the practitioners of the traces, as you call them?! Have you considered how barren the landscape would be without the contributions of the magnificent produc-ers of things and objects among us, of those who make things manifest?! Have you considered the utter blandness in which we would carry our days, the de-spaired lack of meaning that our lives would acquire?! You who speak of tyranny—have you thought of the tyranny that would hold sway if the works of the imag-ination, the works born of sweat and tears, had not left for us, among us, objects that accompany us, that soothe us, that belong to us, that are there, for all to see, marvel at, value and believe and love?! Have you lost your mind, O prophet of tracelessness?! O prophet of the NothingDoings!

O how you err—and O how you mistake my call for another! I have not called for tracelessness all around, I have only told of the works without traces—and this telling, again, is part, *part*, of the Anagraphika. This tell-ing, part of the story—and the story of the telling of the story. See in our attempt the glory of everyday life, the celebration of every moment, of every breath. I have seen the cohorts longing for better. I have seen the cortege of the young artists coming along, now dead. I have seen the corpses on the street, I have heard the cries and the whispers of the lost and the soulless and the weary and the dead. I have seen it all—and I burned even the great works of mine and those of many friends, I promise you—and I began again, I began this, the first artwork, the first of all artworks, perhaps the only artwork I shall ever engage in and tell of: the beginning of all things, before the beginning of all things, *the degree zero of artistic creation*, the DeZA— the degree zero of art! I have not dismissed the past, but overcome it. I have not destroyed the museums, I will shun them. I have not—I will. Fill in the blank!

Hear the call of the liberators! We know, we have known! We sang the praise of art and museums, believe us! We told the crowds and the masses, we clamored and yelled, we promised and hooted the horns! We said come, come and see the attempts at world-making, at reality-making—we were the ones! And now, we set the necessary conditions for a new beginning... Moving on from the trace... Yes, first, life: breathing life into every moment, and towards a new consciousness! A deliverance from the looking and the thinking and the being-with-objects! A deliverance from the grasping at the meaning of life through objects! A deliverance from the worship of objects and their progeny—or of absence, even, and the objects that remind us of absence. A deliverance, from the object being the *reference*. Here, the trace itself is the reference—and we are delivered from *it*, even. A new consciousness: with each step full of life and meaning, a passion unmatched! Every single act, breath, thought, imbued with the force of the making of Anagraphika: of artworks without traces!

And from there, from an early formulation and construction of the Anagraphika, from what was really a prolegomena to the coming triumph, the new works: the NothingDoings! In the beginning was the trace—and we built a new world through the artworks without traces, the Anagraphika! And beyond? A new world, a new consciousness still, a new overcoming, a new totally awesome type of artwork, the grand overcoming, the greatest of victories: the fashioning, and the actual creation, of the NothingDoings. O glorious NothingDoings, O my beloved NoDos, O how we love and embrace you, O O, O beloved NothingDoings! If only the universe of art and the universe of ideas and the universe of actions and the universe of humans knew what you have brought into the world...

O fabulous NothingDoings, how grand is your contribution, O artworks without manifestation *and* without announcements, how marvelous is your proposed impact! O NothingDoings, how delirious, your name, O NothingDoings, how satisfying, your embrace... O NothingDoings, how we shall forever revere you and sing your praises and completely drown in the greatness you bring forth! Forever writing an elegy, forever this ode, to the NothingDoings, to the victory of the NothingDoings!

.

2. The Triumph of the NothingDoings

O beauteous and bountiful world of art! O plentiful realms of art! Thus far, your world has rested upon, inevitably, *appearance*—one of being present, *revealed*. We can speak of all forms, all new forms even, all innovations—stylistic, formal, structural, whatever, in fact: the scenes of art have been one of visibility, or rather, *experiencability*. The entire quiddity of art has rested on the possibility of various subjects experiencing it. All traditional artworks, all challenging works, all innovative works that challenged the traditions, all the avant-garde movements and works even, all of them—they were all *manifest*. We can provide the lists but why bother? One has only to refer to any number of anthologies, catalogues, histories, little volumes even describing the 'isms' of centuries past. From the traditional school to the avant-gardes, from one coast to another, one side of the world to another: all the work is founded upon being present, manifest, announced. How primitive, I'm tempted to say! How old-fashioned even! The idea of a movement! The idea of a new ism! The idea, even, of *doing*. The act of. Doing. Anything. That would allow us to even get to a new ism or a new movement... No, no more... No more of those... Never again...

There is another category, a category unknown to most, a category that I have fashioned that no one knew about, a category that no one *could have* known about, and that radically switched the paradigm of art creation, and of the experience, or lack thereof, of this art. A great category, an almost unimaginable category of artworks that goes beyond the traditional and the vanguards, that radically transforms the very *experiencability* of art. Hallelujah, I almost want to shout (but will withhold) for, lest anyone seek to dismiss this as a novelty or as a 'genre' within a bigger category, we strike back forcefully that it is an *art form*! And the great achievement of this new art form, I say, is that it puts into question perhaps the most major 'seme' of art: it challenges its very *manifestability*.

And I have given this new art form a name, and I have put into motion some of these artworks, yes—they are fantastic and unperceivable pieces! And they do indeed have a name: NothingDoings! Ah the glorious NothingDoings, what pleasure they brought when they were in full swing! These might indeed constitute the bravest of innovations—a most glorious introduction into the realm of art, perhaps one of the few new *relevant* works! Works whose glory and proofs of existence are derived from these very sentences and whose only known 'recognition' is derived from the sentences and the words that might be exchanged from here on out among various readers and cognoscenti...

And thus and so... From the early progeny, the Anagraphika, we moved on to the NothingDoings, works *unmanifest and unannounced* ! Along with the erasure of the necessity of the production of the object, we eliminated the production of non-object-centered works as well, my brethren! Even works that are 'experiences' but are manifest, we eliminated! And further and further, my friends, for I have liberated all from the last vestiges even, the last steps, the artworks *without objects* also *not manifest* but still *announced*. I worked hard and harder and hardest and plowed through and discovered the last, the very last of the possible artworks of liberation, artworks that are not manifest and remain unannounced: the NothingDoings! And a whole array of them, a whole array that will allow you to, well, the verb is missing, I'm not sure which verb to use—make, create, produce, birth, all of the above—fashion, perhaps, fashion artworks that are not manifest and remain unannounced: the NothingDoings, the glorious O forever glorious, NothingDoings.

·

Have you heard the vocabulary that comes out of the mouths of our contemporaries? They use such silly concepts as 'emerging' and 'mid-career' and, ah, I can barely keep up! What odious mechanisms—and to think that the fools play along! Emerging into what?! Mid which career?! Do they not see that they are being defined and directed by the very forces they purportedly fight and challenge?! At least if the pretensions of the battle were not there, and the colleagues claimed they were in it for the money, and even the glory, and just carried on. But no! They claim innovation, they claim intervention! They claim they are challenging and hoping for new world views, and yet, they are, perhaps unbeknownst to them, being played like nice little fools! What frivolousness indeed! And let me assure you generous reader, your era also will have plenty of silly concepts and words and directions associated with its artists. Whether you believe it or not, fight it, challenge it, dismiss it, or not. Have we not, with the Anagraphika and the NothingDoings, spurned the silly questions of 'emerging' vs. 'established' artist, the question of mid-career vs. early or late, have we not destroyed these categories and in the process, sent the clear message that none of these categories indeed are worth considering or taking seriously?! Have we not, in effect, burned in effigy the silly concepts and conceptual frameworks and world views that are handed down, and liberated ourselves and the future generations from the silliness that reigns! We have indeed, and the works without traces and the NothingDoings will leave no concept and no category and no framework and no paradigm and no venture untouched!

Are we mocking the art-market then. Are we mocking the manner in which the players that make up the whole shebang carry along. Are we in the business of such deliberate attempts at undermining a whole range of practices. Why write questions without question marks! Obvious reason: they're not questions! The NothingDoings are less concerned with an attack on establishments and institutions and players and markets than they are with liberty, with deliverance, with the smashing of idols, with *reality-making* and *world-making* and the fashioning of a *new consciousness*! Is it not normal, a given, that such work, with its destruction of categories and frameworks and practices and paradigms, can not help but usher in a whole new manner of being, and undermines and problematizes collecting, selling, buying, the very logic of commerce, economics, and the market?! How can one collect a NothingDoing?! How can one engage in the collection of such artworks?! How can one sell them, how can one buy them?! Imagine the scene at auction: work number twenty two, a work without a trace! Another NothingDoing just went for over a million! Two! Ten! Twenty million! Highest NothingDoing ever sold at auction! The audience in revolt! The chairs that fly! The cries of coming calamities, the cries of the coming tide! The end of life! The end of time! The foundations crumble, the structure crumbles: a world in ruin, a world in ruin!

And in these ruins value is washed away! The concept of value and the way we have fashioned it! Giving value, attaching value! And I'm talking all sorts of value folks: I'm talking emotional, talking psychological, talking cultural, and yes, talking financial value. How to attach, give value to the Anagraphika?! How to attach and give value to a NoDo?! Impossible, unpossible, anpossible!! *Anpossible* : as in, it is a question that is rendered moot! The institutions, the operations, the underlying foundations of value-giving, of value-making all tremble faced with the genius of the Anagraphikal and NothingDoingal unfoldings. All of the nonsensical mannerisms and all the fallacious babblings and all the terror of the financial elite imposing notions and modes of valuation, and scaling, and buying, along with their perpetual rendering of reality in such manner that these operations are continued, perpetuated and glorified, along with their concoction of the tools and mechanisms necessary to concretely propagate this crap all the time (talking money, talking banking, talking all the machines of economic exchange): all of these are targeted, and yes, all are rendered weak, all rendered powerless. The monsters slaughtered! The terrible monsters destroyed, destroyed, destroyed!! And all the institutions that allow such manipulations, such propagations, also destroyed. All washed away, rendered useless in the face of the way the NoDos are fashioned, formed, transformed.

Fear the practitioners of the NothingDoings! And if by reading this one trace/document you thought that we are peaceful partners and practitioners, I say again, fear the practitioners of the NothingDoings, for they are out to destroy all the concepts and the visions of the worshippers of the traces, of the worshippers of the objects and the experiences and the post-experiences. Idol-smashers we remain, and the killers of prophets and of gods—of all stripes, and of all faces. Putting into motion every question that arises, rendering all other questions moot—rendering them moot I say again! And before a world without questions, trembling and unaware and unknowing what to do in the face of these unfoldings, there are no: answers! Hear me well: it is not that there are no answers, it's that there are no: answers. Answers are a foreign entity, unwanted, irrelevant. No questions, no answers—instead, all is an *unfolding*. See the professors and the curators running amok in the streets, hands on heads scramming fearing the death of the gods! Hear them now even the most agnostic among them calling on the gods to save them, and their *jobs*! All businesswomen and men: in the face of the coming of the NothingDoings, running scared into the streets seeking redemption! Where questions and answers have been rendered irrevocably irrelevant, where valuation has taken a turn into the abyss, where the... What is left to do for the guardians of the empire?! O guardians of the empire—this is what is left for them to be told—tremble and kneel now, at the unseen doors of the NothingDoings!

And delivered from the silly precepts of the canons, and of the false, I dare say, false pretexts and pretenses of immortality and mortality, they will forego the battles and the wars and lie down or sleep or sit or drink and be merry! Each moment an eternity, each breath a prolonged celebration that no one has ever imagined. And forget not the poets! Have they not been well-versed in the forms of the NothingDoings?! Yes, some would say, in fact, they are the ones who knew it all before: through absence the eternal presence. And the prophets: they were the progenitors of rules and edicts and laws and tyrannical tenets. Let us save the prophets in turn, let us deliver them, the prophets of the past, from the rules and the laws and the tenets that they bestowed! Let us liberate all their subjects and all the poor folk who have been mired in their millennial grips! Let us save them all! And save the future prophets from the same errors. For even though we call for eternal presence, it is not through trickery, lo, through mythology, lo, through that always clever and practical and O so seductive promise of the Future Return so prominent in all the tyrannical mythologies, no, it is the reverse: it is not through absence, but through works without traces, for one, and the NothingDoings, overall! It is through the Anagraphika, works of art without traces, and the NothingDoings, works of art without manifestation, without announcement, that there is meaning given to every breath. Artworks without traces: Anagraphika! Artworks unmanifest and unannounced: NothingDoings! Hallelujah, O NothingDoings!

No more archives, no more dust, no more retrieval of a thing in and of itself, for the thing has been transformed, along with the time. This is not a mystical world view, nor is it art for the sake of some sort of mysticism. Nor is it metaphysics. Nor is it integrating mysticism into art. It is a very specific endeavor that reveals the inadequacy of language. At one point, here, we are stuck about how to talk about it all, the inadequacy of our way of being and relating and identifying. Is this a rant, then? Is this the eleventh-hour plea of a madman, or a failed painter, or a failed artist? Make not the mistake, my friends, this is no rant or roar or plea or pleasantry! Not the frivolous frolicking of a disassembled, dislocated freak no, not the crazy and preposterous cry of a lost soul! Not even musings or diaries or meditations or contemplations or any other among the silly attempts at telling of solitude or aloneness, no! None of the above! I promise the reader: this writer is in the midst of life, on top of his many powers, and yes, on top of his game. A celebrator of life! He carries along with great smiles and smells the flowers and greets passersby and bends down and pets the dogs even. He is vigorous and exercises and contemplates and meditates and enjoys the simple pleasures of life. He oft partakes of the excesses of modern life even and enjoys watching some football and some brainless reality TV shows like the rest of us. Trust him, he is no naysayer or embittered soul, quite the contrary: a merry soul merrier still through the great discoveries and the drowning in the practice of the NothingDoing. He could carry on undaunted, producing magnificent and marvelous objects, so many things and objects that the world would not know what to do with! Enough to fill all the museums of the world with the most beauteous, magnificent collections of artworks! A most cherished artist of the age and of all ages he could become, mired in the same forms of object worship, knee-deep and soon waist-deep and soon even worst, neck-deep, in all the, say it loud say it clear, freaking crap that the many institutions and lords and kings and worlds have imposed! Such silly fetishes with objects, with traces, with materiality, such uncouth considerations as monetary value or immortality. Showiness—ah what garbage truly! No to all that, seriously—goodbye to all that!

And I repeat: this is the one document, the only document, ethereal as can be too, but still, agreed, betraying (slightly) the essential non-quiddity of the Nothing-Doings. Necessary only at the urging of my inner being and friends I repeat, I promise you, they were the ones who hollered and insisted and clamored and shouted and pouted and pulled: you must at least have the one document, the one telling of the early Anagraphika, the one for the NothingDoings! But will that not undermine the very tenet of the Anagraphika and the NoDos, I insisted, or its anti-tenet, not to mention the heart and soul?! Is not the manifesto of the Anagraphika and the NothingDoings not to be written ever, not to mention a manifesto that makes sure it is not manifest?! Must not the Anagraphika and all the NoDos not leave any trace of themselves, must we all not know of them, never know of them? Yes, yes, they said, yes, but you are the one who tells of the telling! You are the one who tells of how that Anagraphika is also the unfolding that it is, the unfolding that it always becomes, a telling of the story of Anagraphika! Consider it another thread in the telling, they said. Another among the platforms of the telling, among the voices of the telling: the telling of the story of the early Anagraphika, the first of the NothingDoings really, the first of what became the NoDos—in the same vein an unfolding, brazen, joyous and flowing. Let it be told, here also, this is the one trace, this is the *only* trace. I insist then, still insist, even with this document being read by you: I have put an end to the worship of, or the collection of, objects. And also to the fashioning of non-object-centered art that remains manifest and announced. I have ushered in the non-objects that are also not manifest and remain unannounced—save for this one doc!

·

With one stroke, I have delivered the future poets, the future painters, the future prophets, the future genii of our time, from the horrendous *expectations and limitations* that this woebegone society has imposed on

them all! I have saved them from the tyranny of that odi-
ous consideration: production, and immortality through
production! They will walk along the same dark alleys
the poets, but they will say about me: that fool saved
our lives! That fool saved us from the devils! That fool
saved us from the deluge! And they will thank me in
the only way the *maudit* poets have ever known: they
will enter houses of ill repute, and using my name as
they wallow in whatever form of delectable debauch-
ery they can find, they'll whisper, if it were not for him,
we would not be so free—but still in the grips of the
thoughts of production and immortality! Ah, they will
hum, glory be to you, lost poet and prophet who saved
us from the fall with the NothingDoings! The painters in
their studios shall forgo the hours of madness and re-
bellion—and sing and praise the NoDos and shout out,
Glory be to you O sage of the NoDos! How forthrightly
you saw the world, how futile the works of centuries
past, how fabulous your discovery! Bravo, the chorus
will go on, bravo to the NothingDoings! Hallelujah, hal-
lelujah to the NoDos!

I have succeeded in fulfilling the ultimate ambition of
all creators: I have made a *new reality*, so uncompro-
mising, so utterly unbecoming of all the silly challeng-
es that will be thrust its way, that it will forever bear the
mark of the prophecy it has indeed proven to be. The
cynical will snicker. The jealous ones will, worse, raise

a ruckus maybe, or even threaten and attack me. A world that will stand the ravages of time, better than any and all that have ever been conceived, presented, fabricated! The world of images forever retained: unformed, yet always transformed.

I have eliminated the object—eternally erased its hold on the psyche! I have destroyed the *last, and only real*, monster that has ever taken hold of our imaginations: *the object*! The one horrendous fetish that is the object, I have forever slayed it! What will we say to the destroyer of our most cherished fetish?! Shall you celebrate the work of this savior that I am?! Consider me your savior my brethren, for with the destruction of the artistic object too, I am liberating the lot of us from the tyranny of artistic beginnings and artistic ends! Do you hear how I have erased all beginnings and ends! Do you hear how I have slashed the tyranny of beginnings and ends! The dragons that are the beginnings and ends! All is flow, repeat after me: all is flow, and in the fabric of the works without traces, the light of the flow shines brightest, the flow becomes the essence, the one constantly transforming site, and un-site, where the images that I capture—yes, they are captured— forever retain their full autonomy, magic and marvel. I capture them, my friends, and liberate them again in the same space of their capturing! How liberating the works without traces are! To give life to the writings of light, to the writing that is a trace! Life, again, eternal life, to its fullest, its truest, its only honest iteration! Celebrate me, for I have liberated us from the tyranny of beginnings and ends, of the fetish of objecthood! I have made the flow the work: the flow the space, the flow the site, the flow the unending road, the flow the path, the flow the god, the flow, the work, the flow the dream, the flow the flow, the flow the flow, the flow, life.

I have achieved what artists for millennia, and the millennial artists, were incapable of achieving: I have made the archive irrelevant. The archive that got to have such a wondrous makeover too, with the advent of the technological breakthrough, the internet, the computer, the machines of the new age. I have rendered the archive more than irrelevant—I have, in fact, made it meaningless: for retrievability, formfulness, contour, tactility, all the many activities associated with the object have been forever transformed, through the very quiddity, or a-quiddity, through the very nature, or a-nature, through the very essence, or an-essence, of the NothingDoings. No more memory, no more study, no more documenting of the inglorious, no more return or retrievals. I have ushered in a *new conjugation of being*, literally, a new way of living the present and what we call the past and the future: the works constantly changing, with the times, with the images, with the very essence of our passage.

And thus the chant must go up: Glory be to the Nothing-Doings! Yes indeed! Glory be to the Anagraphika that paved the way for the glorious NothingDoings! Glory be to this lifestyle, to this relationship with the world, to this relationship to fashioning worlds. Glory be to the NothingDoings! Glory be to the NothingDoings! I repeat. Onward ho! Onward towards a new typology, a typology of the NothingDoings! A new wave of Art! A new way of Life! Glory be to the NothingDoings!

And then another shout and then whispers abounding: O NothingDoings, glory be to you forevermore...

C. The Complete

Inventory of

the NothingDoings

(A Documentary in the Form of a Prose Narrative)

Your aspiring friends and hosts should rest assured that they will find their own paths to the blissful lands of NothingDoings. The best way, I remind you, is to practice. The best way to enter that realm, that is, is to practice it. Practice IT, wink wink. That means, there is no entrance with undue doing. I leave you with these riddles, which are really just one: does the one who seeks to reach the NoDo universe of bliss, actually ever reach it? In other words, does seeking get you there? Or is this The Great Paradox of NoDo-hood: you will get there when you master not-seek-ing, when you practice not-doing. Let them know these wisdoms who seek to join, my fellow NoDoists. Let them know in spurts. Do not overwhelm them. Let them get to it on their own. That is all for now. Coffee sip needed.

From <u>The Book of NoDo</u>
(Meditations on the Mount, 30.2)

(The exchange is thought to have occurred, accord-ing to legend, when a young NoDo pilgrim on the path had beckoned the deacon of NoDohood at the time to explain how one attains the ideal stages of NoDohood, whereupon the NoDo Sage is reported to have offered the words above, with the following

opening: I will consider this important query of yours from my mountain meditation post, otherwise known as 'stool at coffee shop' since I will be 'working from home' today!)

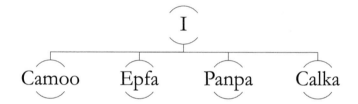

1. Camoo

(The Last Iteration of the Camouflart Pieces)

They are listed first but perhaps they should be listed last—or not at all. Indeed, I've had quite the ambiguous relationship to the NothingDoing/Camoo, for they were, in the beginning, almost fused—or rather, confused—with the NothingDoings themselves. Ah the 'camouflart' pieces, how I dubbed them then, and how I loved them so... Pieces that were hidden, camouflaged, where the audience didn't know they were in fact an audience, where the artworks unfolded with no announcement, without any follow-up or exchange or re/cognition. How fantastic indeed was my love affair with the camouflart pieces!

Soon enough though, I recognized and accepted that the camouflart pieces were indeed manifest, and that works of the camouflaged persuasion could unfold in any number of environments, with any number of characteristics. It was thus not that one said goodbye to the camouflart, just that they happened, in multiple forms and multiple masks, and under different names, in other locales.

The NothingDoing camouflart pieces—the NoDo/ Camoo as they have come to be known—are thus a different species, fully ensconced in the poetics of the NothingDoings. Whereas in the beginning, the camouflart pieces' camouflage characteristic resided in the audience not knowing that an artwork was taking place and that they were participating—thus, the artwork being truly camouflaged—the NoDo/Camoo situates the 'camouflage' aspect within the very fact of unmanifestability: a logical extension of the camouflart poetics, a fuller and more extreme *treatment*, one could say. In the most unexpected of fashions then, in the least probable manner, it remained *hyper*-camouflaged—never making an appearance, never becoming manifest.

•

There is precedence, yes, there always is... And were we not among those who willfully and excitedly participated in the types of artworks that one could easily call the brethren of the Camoos? Yes indeed... I would not call them 'inspirations', but certainly I think of them as worthy parallels, their progenitors as well-meaning pilgrims wandering along similar paths, one could say, and their practitioners as well-meaning folks authentically preoccupied with similar problematics, friends we shall always salute along the way—friends though, whose ideas and worthy challenges we overcame, finders as we are, of new paths and new lives.

First, let us speak of the works that invited *disintegration*: the work itself disintegrating through the material, as it were, or a work that would be put through destruction by its makers, or by others, or by watchers or participants. Beyond the progressive destruction, dismantling, disintegration of an œuvre, I think of a second cousin to the NoDo/Camoos: those works that relied on the progressive disavowal of an œuvre: *discontinuation*, as it were, as an art form itself, whether only announced—with that announcement forming the foundations of the ongoing lack of doing a work—or an actual allowance for a manifest form of discontinuation through material manipulation or lack thereof—that is, a discontinuation visible and tactile and experiencable, accompanied by the visible enacting, or erecting, of ruins. I am proud of many that I created myself, yes, however soft my whisper... I must also give a *chapeau* to a species of artists that we know well, and who have acquired quite legendary status in many domains. We are speaking, of course, of the *artistes sans œuvre*, these fascinating and misunderstood creatures who have forever tugged at my lonesome heart! They were mentioned at length in the preface, and we do indeed feel the affinity. All these distant cousins of the NoDoist engage either 1) in the creation of an absence of a visible or manifest work, through that work's a) disintegration/destruction or b) discontinuation, or 2) in the never-launched presence and thus perpetually absent 'work' of the *artiste sans œuvre*. And yet, they all still participate in the 'scene' whereby art is *manifest*—invisible perhaps, or disappearing, or turning into ruins or never becoming present—as an *absence*: manifest as *an absence following a presence* in the case of both a) the disintegration/destruction works and b) the discontinuation works; or absent as such, and *present in that announced perpetual absence*, in the case of the works (meaning, absence of works) of the *artistes sans œuvre*.

The NothingDoing/Camoo were hard-to-conceive yet definitely unmanifest and unannounced pieces, in harmony with the essence of the NothingDoings. Works at a pre-camouflage state, as it were, or a hyper-camouflaged state: where the camouflagedness is at the extreme point of a spectrum, works that are unmanifest and unannounced, yet ever lively, ever *there*!

·

I write in the past tense when it comes to the Camoo

I do... The NoDo/Camoo have come and gone, been fashioned, and have been *forever eradicated* through this very articulation of their once-upon-a-time *existence*. I repeat: because of the very nature of the Camoo, resting upon a secret camouflagedness, the Camoo have now been rendered obsolete. This writing, these sentences, have assured their death. Not only are those particular (and titled) works of Camoo forever gone and unrepeatable, but the fact of creation of more has now also been rendered impossible. It is the *entire category of NoDo/Camoo* that has been rendered impossible with the revelation of the existence of this very category, and the fact of certain artworks that existed under its aegis having unfolded in reality.

Thus, not only will none of the actual realized NoDo/Camoo ever be put into motion again, but there will be no more works ever again fashioned under the category 'camouflart' since the 'camoufl' part of the art form has been outed, revealed. Not only NoDo/Camoo, but the entire panoply and spectrum. With this writing, with the very graphing of these words on paper (yes, paper), prior to the reader even reading them but assuredly after, camouflart pieces have irrevocably been rendered obsolete. A death happy, I must write. A death worthwhile. A death life-affirming more than any other—that confirms, a life. That otherwise would not have been known. A death that reveals the life.

Camouflarts: lives brought to the fore, reality rendered differently, and the withering away, quickly in a way, of the same realities...

•

2. Epfa

(Ex Post Facto Art)

On a walk in the park with Sagóbaksha Shahóvar, I be-
gan to expound on the concept of a certain type of art-
work, namely those works that were not perceived as
such (as 'work' or as 'art' and ultimately as 'artwork') at
the moment of their doing. 'I'm not sure I have ever en-
countered the concept,' I told her politely, meaning, in
effect, nobody's done this before! I added: 'Although,
admittedly, based on the very *type of work* that it is, it
is possible that we would never actually know of it...'

Sago (for short) says: 'You mean you're going to do
stuff that's not called art that you'll later call art?' Enam-
ored and smiling, she was, and perhaps justifiably so,
not taking issue with the content of my position or the
very fact that I was espousing it too seriously—and just
enjoying a sunny day and a pleasant conversation and
company. Not quite I say, I'm saying that I would like to
bestow the characteristic of artness, and, I insist, based
on some solid theoretical grounds, upon a number of

'stuff'—and I say 'stuff' because they can range from objects to phenomena to rituals etc. that occurred in the past. Since I'm doing nothing other than bestowing in that way a 'status' and thus simply re-perceiving and re-categorizing objects and events, I dub my actions, and the overall type of artwork that is generated, as another NothingDoing. And, for good measure, the subcategory is *Ex Post Facto Art*. She laughs, stops and turns to me: 'You're serious?!?' she says. Dead, I say—dead serious. And I will call it the Epfa!

Surprisingly, as she begins to take the next step (leading me to the same), she turns and says: 'I like it. Like it a lot! Very liberating!' Well, thank you, I say, I agree. Plus, it's cool and innovative, really is. And although I intend to do it mostly with my own stuff, there's no reason to not do it with other people's stuff. Or other entities. Could be institutions. Groups. Collectives. From long ago and/or faraway. 'Can they do it on their own,' she asks? You mean, the NoDo/Epfa? Yes, they can do the same. I presume, I said, if anyone can do a painting, why couldn't everyone do an Epfa? I paused and began to reconsider. It's actually subtle and nuanced, I said, so it's critical to know what you're doing. I smiled: 'It takes decades of work and experience to be able to do it right!'

·

We jumped straight to the Epfas, for I wanted to see where in the panoply of practices of this type of re-categorization the Epfas themselves fell. Indeed, since multiple re-categorizations can be conceived, we decided to cite two that readily come to mind. She understood and we spoke in general during our casual stroll and ended up somehow focusing on those two particular ones, which we thought probably most pertinent, especially when it came to practices that potentially could challenge the art world categories. 1. The first was a general umbrella that itself included two subcategories, namely: a) *Unaware Art*, or haphazard art: when something has been done *to* something—i.e. operations (like cuts) wrought upon posters that give an interesting result; and b) *Chance Art*—i.e. light falling on buildings for example (which is, by the way, very different from using *chance phenomena to create new things then classified as art*). One could potentially conceive of documenting these even, and integrating them within a body of work. (In both of these cases, I continued, we might even consider types of works that constitute something akin to an *Assisted Nothing-Doing*. A suggestion I quickly dismissed because if not wholly a NoDo, then there could be no NoDo! And thus, as seductive as an 'Assisted NoDo' seemed, it simply could not be part of the NoDo universe!) 2. The second general category along these lines is what comes close to being E*x Post Facto Art*, where subsequent to the passage of time (any amount), an action or ritual or experience or thing or project, is *re-conceptualized as having constituted an artwork*. That is: nothing new is fashioned, but a mental or scriptural operation re-categorizing the nature of something is put into place.

•

We continued to walk and talk about the finer points of the Epfa. In the process of bringing to the fore concepts related to the Epfa, we recognized that the new work I was speaking of—the newly-acquiring-the-status-of-art work—was leading me to fashion a 'manifest' work. In announcing the now-turned-into-artwork stuff, we were the progenitors of a 'new' entity, made of old stuff. Even though it was a recycling of sorts—not of the material of an object into another object, but the recycling of the same 'thing/experience' from one type or category into another (art)—it was still bestowing artness on an old existing object/experience/ritual etc. The actual NoDo, then, to be precise was the *pre*-new-object phase, *the culling and the finding* of the stuff that was going to be recycled, and *the turning-it-over to the Epfa mechanisms*. That, really, IS the Epfa, that is the NoDo artwork, that is the NoDo/Epfa. The old 'stuff' that had now turned into an artwork is not itself the Epfa.

To diminish confusion, then, it was important to distinguish the phases and the nomenclature: the final form of the new artwork, the object/experience/event/ritual etc. that had turned into an artwork would be, in effect, something else, including, very possibly, an existing category of art. The NothingDoing/Epfa had to do with *the process of bequeathing, the process of finding and re-categorizing*. Bequeathing the status of art on works that were *not intended to be artworks*, but that, upon further review—or the passage of time—fall under that glorious etiquette, is a surreptitiously worthy undertaking, we agreed. Haphazard events that totally fall into the category of art based on a number of criteria established as constituting a work of art, allows the categorizer, the re-categorizer, to see and perceive the world differently. Perhaps even more fabulously, it allows all concerned to *re-quiddify* the thing or event that had not been perceived as such, thus allowing it to *ascend* to, *transform* into its new quiddity. Not due to anything other than: a discovery of a better theory of what constitutes art, or a new theory of art that did not exist at the time, or to the development of new art forms since the appearance of the thing now arranged under Epfa. Thus, the re-quiddifying—which, in singular fashion, does not bring any change to the world, or add any *products*—still contributes to the world of art, constitutes, what is more, a new art.

•

Who would the audience be, the question was, and when would they experience these? Was it just as excursions—as coming-to-being through conversation—without any further *concretization*? Or was there a show, in the future, dubbed *Ex Post Facto: Phenomena, Rituals, Objects, and Other Whatnots Now Categorized as Art*? Solo show? Group show? Would I be the curator? Was this supposed to continue and carry on? Was this conversation supposed to be expanded? Questions answered? New questions posed? New queries formulated? What was on that list anyway?

'You're driving me crazy,' she said. 'Why can't we just talk about, I don't know, paintings, or installations?' She laughed and I, now on an adrenaline rush, began to list some of the actual Epfas. I continued the banter and even selected 'stuff' of others and re-arranged them. The operation of the bestowing of artness rests upon the general awareness to perceive, capture, and document events, objects, and other phenomena differently, and the readiness to go ahead with the re-categorization, I continued theoretically. Indeed, the most crucial point here was that the minimal operation of the arting—*the re-categorization*—was based on the bequeathing of authority on the self, or any other entity doing the arting. When we had come upon the place we had started our conversation—our walk had taken us one time around the pond of the small park in which we were strolling—we decided that an abrupt ending was most appropriate. That indeed was it. That.

.

3. Panpa

(The Political Act of Non-Participation and Protest)

The political act of non-participation has had many avatars throughout the years. In action, in institutions, in societal venues. Civil disobedience. Rights of refusal. Certain activistic credos. Our own 'Abandonment' projects. Yes indeed. The NothingDoings did not begin as a purely political species. In fact, the idea—acknowledged by us—that politics is a *part* of any artwork was somehow not fully *appreciated* by us, even though we, among most, are those who consider all artworks, given the nature of form, structure, style, to be political. We managed somehow, perhaps in an embrace of irony and the absurd, perhaps in a desire to further develop the NothingDoing, to do nothing at all politically. That is, in a desire for the NothingDoing to have *no attributes*, to be devoid of all types and manners of characteristics, we neglected to recognize its great *politicalness*. Somehow in looking for the fabulous glory of the NothingDoings as pure and emblematic artworks (again, NothingDoing *as an artwork* is *not* the

art of doing nothing), we probably purposefully decid-
ed to not attach it to a decidedly politically weighted
and anarchistic endeavor. But...

But soon enough, the invitation, the imposition, came
through the NoDos themselves. Were they not, after
all, fabulous forms of the political act of non-participa-
tion in action? This type of the NoDo, I dare say, was
among the most daring, the most innovative type of
political act of non-participation—in being a non-act,
or an *a-act*, in action: among peers, in institutions, in
industries, in disciplines and in 'worlds', such as the
art world, the philosophy world etc... Non-participation,
non-acknowledgment—a veritable form of protest. A
most potent form of protest. A most authentic and un-
compromised form of protest.

·

If other varieties of NothingDoings steer clear of identi-
fication with this strand of political action, perhaps em-
bodying it but to lesser degrees and not as the main
thrust, the NoDo/Panpa retains its legitimate and jus-
tified existence within the panoply of NoDos on the
horizon. It just so happens that this type of NoDo also
hopes to achieve recognition as *a form of protest*, and
thus, as opposed to many other NoDos, *calls attention
to itself*, makes itself relevant (if retaining, with much

effort, its unmanifestness) as the subject of conversation—albeit in quite irregular ways. (And we can only imagine the ways in which the protest form of NoDo will affect the other NoDos and vice-versa.) It is unimaginable that this form will not continue—with the challenge being the manner in which it draws attention to itself. Perhaps the NoDo/Panpa just makes various factions of the populace *aware of it*, and the ways in which it is hoping to *intervene*.

Surely, the day will come when a new vocabulary will also greet the world relative to the way protests and actions are undertaken—or not. The Panpa may become a household word, and 'panping' a gerund used often to refer to certain forms of a-action in the political sphere. *Panping*, in effect, will become part of the overall toolkit of the great NoDoists. One of the ways in which they will be able to carry along in life, stay true to their general NoDo practice, and fashion the political version of the unmanifest and unannounced artwork, the NoDo/Panpa.

It is entirely possible that these panpaic pioneers will be mocked, and surely in a time where activism takes on very particular flavors, namely, a certain loudness and a certain visibility. Certainly shunned, for, in the political sphere especially, being announced, visible, manifest, trump all other characteristics. But the answer perhaps lies therein, in the 'owning' up to that very condition: the Panpa must remain a NoDo, and thus continue to embrace its characteristics. That is as it should be. We be panpers, might become the chant. But, alas, it will be a silent chant, unheard and unmanifest. But perhaps not unperceived.

For we are convinced that everywhere, there are many who ascribe to the glory of the NoDos, and who are just as enthralled with the lifestyle it allows, and just as enamored with the Panpa—secret panpers they may even be, and showing them the way, somehow, is all it might take. And then the panpers of the world will unite, and the panpers of the world will dance, and the panpers of the world will sing and drink to the glory of futures forever brighter. Yes, they will. Or else, not.

·

4. Calka

(Beyond the Calque)

I remember in the galleries O how I remember in the galleries how during a most memorable lecture to the assembled, I told them enthusiastically of the Nothing-Doing/Calka. How it was that, upon further and further exploration of the stature and nature of the aesthetic experience, and what it was that we expected from it, I had decided to label some of the activities I was engaged in as *art*. The entire conversation had launched where, quite predictably, one member among said assembled, enraged at one of the pieces on display and how it constituted art, had exclaimed: 'Who decides this?! Who decides this is art?!' Whereupon I had answered, calmly, coolly, with a devilish grin on my visage, with the question, 'What are your expectations, sir, of what constitutes art?' Whereupon he had considered the question and answered, since now the onus was on him. Whereupon a conversation had ensued, he had calmed down, and I had digressed into what I am now recounting.

I had decided to share, that is, with this group, this enthused group attending the revered museum, the considerations that had gone through my head most recently regarding what I had formulated as the New Banalism—or, 'the doing of all things banal as art'—and how it had quite strong theoretical foundations and could in fact be considered quite the funky paradigm-shifter. I told the assembled of the fundamentals and the foundations of the new art, and I gave them examples. I told them how I had fashioned other names for it, given those up, branded it anew, given those up too, and from there focused only on its characteristics, allowing the name itself to be irrelevant, and, well, banal.

I told them of how I had considered and then formulated quite strongly in theoretical terms, but without undulily burdening anyone with these theories, the foundations of this movement. I then gave some examples. How as I was walking down the street, the act of walking down the street constituted art. My sitting at a table was art. My standing waiting for the bus was art. All this, again, I could demonstrate with rigor (through equations almost if necessary), relative to *the legacy of certain types of artworks*, and *a mapping of the direction of certain art movements* and where on that map this type of action would fall: what *art historical lineage*, in other words, it would follow, and how it was an *innovative extension of certain trajectories in art*—one in which I was, granted, recharting, rewriting, revising the history of art through new categories. In other words, a *radical remapping* of the relevant isms and movements and works—that is, the creation of new isms based on the new categories and thus a new mapping, where the 'relevant' and paradigm-shifting works would obviously be different—would also allow the placement of my new type of artwork as a relevant new branch on my new map of isms and schools of thought. Yes, for all those subtle enough to wonder, this necessitated, and did indeed put into motion, and action, and finalization, without hubris or excessive self-aggrandizement, but without hesitation as well or timidity, a new way of writing the history of art, a new, lo, history of art *tout court*.

My new work was not dubbed art through the oft-quoted and O so terribly cliché idea that 'it is art when I label it so' (a worthy position I am sympathetic to but not entirely convinced of in any case), but from the maneuvering and displacing of the parameters of the form— that is, of performance, of films, of the image in movement etc... Subscribing to my aesthetic position—not a fundamentalist immovable ideal but one that I seemed to return to over and over—I submitted that *the shifting of an element of the parameters of the form allowed this innovation within artistic practice to take place*. In certain works, for example, I was combining a performance *without* an audience (instead of *with*) with the use of a *cameraless* film to concoct a number of works that made the activity of the every day to be re-cast, with very strong theoretical foundations, as art. Or, in a reverse move, I could participate in any number of daily activities and simply imagine a combination of operational moves on the parameters of particular art forms that would allow whatever I was doing, under my own theoretical inclinations, to be considered art. And where a defense was necessary of why whatever I was classifying as art could thus be classified, I could simply concoct and talk about, on the spot, the manipulations of certain parameters of recognized and accepted art forms and strongly argue for how the operations at work were fashioning the new art form I was creating—the one I was defending.

•

Well, lo and behold, as oft occurs, I discover soon enough that something similar to the New Banalism has indeed been done before—not necessarily based on the same arguments or poetics or aesthetics no, but leading to very similar results. Soon enough, the discovery is confirmed with more research: that along these lines a large number of practitioners had moved, each giving a different hue, a different signature to the venture. This, then, is where I had left New Banalism, I was telling the by-now rapt audience who had quite fascinatingly forgotten the works adorning the walls of the revered museum and were entranced by my account of the progress of the creation of a new artistic form. They wanted me to continue and I did not hold back. I told them of the progress of the movement after the discoveries, and how the itinerary took on a new shape whereupon I, the practitioner/theorist, was genuinely in the throes of fashioning something singular, arriving at a better formulation indeed. They were excited to hear, and they assured me that this exchange was much more interesting than a regular observation and discussion of the 'classics' on the walls. (Those among them who did not agree with this change of direction in our exchange were free to leave, and they did.)

In the universe of the NothingDoings, I began to expound, a subcategory that I happily label the 'Calque' was being birthed, what I humorously had dubbed the 'Canodo' at first, and finally, the 'Calka'. The presentation of the Calka necessitated a swift grounding in the aesthetics of the NothingDoings, and this I offered in a manner most impressive, and with everyone sitting on the ground of the gallery, assembled in a circle. After fielding certain puzzled questions about the Nothing-Doings as such, and after puzzled queries were answered to the satisfaction of the doubters, and after enlivened protests were held in check—that is, after all had satisfactorily been updated on the nature of the NothingDoings as a general category of art forms (without, of course, going into detail about certain types)—we agreed that we would expound on the NothingDoing/Calka.

The Calka was quite subtly yet importantly different from the earlier formulations of works belonging to my short-lived New Banalism, I offered—those works that one could legitimately call 'banalistic' art, those that came to be through the re-categorization of certain actions and activities *as* art with strong arguments within the legacy of the movements and history of artworks. Rather than re-position, or re-imagine, or re-classify an existing and *occurring* act as the artwork, the Calka, I offered insistently, can consist of *concocted calques* of the everyday—that is, not the actual thing that one is doing, but a *calque*—which also *must occur* in those situations that such actions would occur, but with subtle, nuanced variations that made them stand out, but not so much that they would be perceived as artwork. All the components of these nuances are important: what appears as regular then is *not*, but is an infinitesimal shift away from being the regular occurrence. In this case, then, as opposed to both a) other NoDos where the re-categorization itself fashions the work and b) similar works that could re-imagine the everyday occurrence as art (the original works within New Banalism), the shift of doing the very thing that one could do at times but with slight variations is the NoDo.

•

I hear you already friends of galleries past, I exclaimed to the patient listeners, but, hear me: that is the point, the very puzzlement that you so legitimately seem to be communicating is at the foundation of this Nothing-Doing. That slight shift is not much. The move away, not much. The Calka is a figurative French *calque* AND *claque* (slap) of sorts! Do these Calkas not constitute, in effect, just an illusion, an excuse, a way of responding to the charge of these types of works already appearing on the artistic landscape? No, we say, they do not. For, who, ever, could prove that the calque was not the real thing?! Who would be measuring?! Who would be ascertaining that the parameters I just described for the Calka were actually at play?! No, my friends, the Calka is, in the best tradition of the NothingDoing, a ruse: the great work of the trickster, a NoDo master-work indeed! Let us repeat: a *calque* and a *claque*!

I was surprised at the reaction of the group (no member of which I ever saw again, and from whom no other response I ever received), one that, for good measure I must detail. (And by the way, the content of that mo-

mentous exchange I had never shared again, or artic-
ulated, anywhere, until now!) The reaction was the fol-
lowing: they rose almost as if in a trance, and began to
applaud wildly, standing and swaying and applauding,
no one saying a word, the circle around me, I in the
center, almost as if a ritual, bringing to a standstill the
other galleries of the museum, turning the attention of
all the other museum-goers to our circle, we now the
focal point, this, perhaps, an artwork in and of itself,
this, the perfect example of the proposed NoDo, this
the demonstration, most exemplary demonstration, of
the essence, the power, and the force, and the sin-
gularity and the importance and the relevance, of the
NothingDoing/Calka.

•

II

One day, The Great Fog will be lifted
and the masses of NoDo initiates
will walk (or not) towards the beach,
where they will lay down and bask in the sun.
Out of the Do closet—at last.

From The Book of NoDo
(Sayings of the Guides, 20.1)

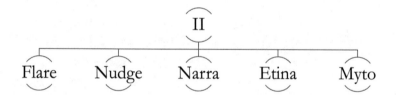

5. Flare

We dare not say it—and perhaps we should not say it: the work that surprises and shocks, that seemingly innocuous work that out of nowhere thrusts itself into the daily fabric of our lives, that work that conforms to that most aesthetic of effects—meaning, it jolts us out of the humdrum rhythm of the everyday—that work that suddenly in the midst of the crowd forces the crowd to think anew about its relationship to the world, that imposes upon the world to question its assumptions—those flames, those flames, those panicked faces, those sudden dashes away and the shrieks and the coordinated multi-sited attack, attack of the senses only, one would hope, but, alas, it might well be an attack on the edifice, on the customs, on the very way of life—that work that makes everyone stop and talk and scream and bemoan, and so seldom, so seldom question their positions, that work, so omnipresent in our lives, that makes the crowds gather at the unexpected climbing of a pole in a heavily populated area, whereupon the climber screams and shouts, those works where the entire movements of our lives come under scrutiny and question if we allowed them, those works that point to the silliness of all the other artistic creations, that point to the self-absorbedness and ir-relevance of so much artistic production, that point to the inability of the regularly labeled 'artworks' to *surprise* and *jolt* us *out*, those works that directly shake us into recognizing the terra-totally-not-firma on which we stand and that can indeed be fashioned in utter-ly unexpected ways—perhaps significantly because they are *not presented as artworks*—those works that like flares among us appear, if only we knew how to perceive them, how to read them as such, read them right, and re-categorize them even, those works that have us in awe upon their unexpected encounter, and prompt us to sigh and think: they are where it's at: and *this* is the artwork: the NothingDoing/Flare... Ahhh, the NothingDoing/Flare... No more sighs, for, that very si-lent and personal and meditative cognition and recog-nition, that is a type of new NoDo: the Flare...

•

Let us cite one of the more recent examples of the NothingDoing/Flare. In the summer of 2013, we are walking in the 'zócalo' of Mexico City, whereupon we come upon the tents, the makeshift protesters' en-campments—and the many activities that come with the territory— and the sights, the colors, the sounds, the noises, the movement, the choreography of chaos and anger and madness and protest. Brujas and doctors of the witch kind, warriors and their modern incarnations, screaming faces and babies asleep in the arms of their shouting mothers with toddlers hand in hand marching along. We are not judging, hear us, the merits or demerits of what is called a protest, we are pointing to the *experience* that we had—and in its sublime format: the conglomeration of sounds and sights all around, enveloping us, transforming our experience of the world, transforming our understanding of the connections of things and phenomena in the world, forcing us to walk a certain way, run, duck, go under the hanging lines or skip over the flame—experiencing the same space in an entirely new way, and in a completely unexpected manner. No, we care not about the de/merits of the protest, or of the calls, only about the radical shift of perception wrought upon our being, and the radical change of the experience of the space, of the day—all *not* under the guise of art. We care that this ensemble, not presented as art, became just that, a NothingDoing/Flare.

We dare not say, but we must, and we have: the art of now, is it not the *actual* subversive acts of resistance? Is it not the hidden dashes and clashes and the impromptu rebellions? This work, this art, *not labeled so by its progenitors*, by its practitioners: this art de-mands spectatorship, and participation. This art is *not participatory*, but the opposite: we *ordain it as artwork* while we are spectators and deem it *theee* artwork! In turning ourselves into willing watchers and spectators bequeathing upon these irrepressible *flares* among us a new status, we honor and prize these ubiquitous joltings-out of our humdrum existence, and thus fash-ion another species of NothingDoing. The simultane-ous attack of the compound; the multi-site invasion; the coordinated killing of insurgents; the protests and shouts and repetitions of lines and the die-ins and the hands up don't shoot. We are agents of the NoDo becoming through the bequeathing of spectatorship and the turning of that spectatorship *into* an artwork in and of itself. The variety of NothingDoing dubbed Flare, then, consists of the 'reading' of these events *as modern-day artworks of the most powerful signifi-cance* through the *positioning of one as a spectator*, and the *transformation of that spectatorship itself into the aesthetic/sublime experience that it is*. Nothing doing other than through the rendering of one self a spectator, *through the very fact of becoming spectator and bequeathing artness on the event*.

There is indeed something majestic about the Nothing-Doing/Flare: the constructs of humans in coherent ac-tion with their desires and their ambitions, an *authentic* act in the world, a *violent* act, in many ways, because it not only interferes in the sphere of life, but undermines the timidity of regular artwork—the garden variety that one finds in galleries and museums. No, the temerity, the ferociousness of the intervention is beyond the realm of the artist. And the courage displayed beyond the usual bland cacophony of the intellectuals. These are the *relevant* works of our time, and at the expert hand of the NoDoist, they can turn into powerful works of our times: the NothingDoing/Flare.

·

6. Nudge

In the galleries of a space we stumble upon today, the types of things one always sees: works on the walls, works on the floors, a few on a pedestal, and some even hanging. Today though, a peculiarity, due to the fact that there was, obviously, a little gathering of folks, for there are traces of this gathering: a small table with a white tablecloth atop; a tray that would have been full of bagels now empty save for a few morsels here and there; the coffee 'container'—the portable thing one sees at all such gatherings; the similarly bland container of hot water; a small tray of stirrers; a stack of napkins. Remnants and traces of what seemed a work gathering without pretention at the edge of the gallery: absence personified, a photograph itself.

In the midst of the artworks in the gallery, this assemblage—literally an assemblage of objects and not a type of artwork—stands out at an emotional level: an innocent reminder, a sign, of human activity and exchange. But it also stands out as a *possible artwork*, had it been intended as such, *while simultaneously* making one aware that it is specifically this *accidental presence*, and *the lack of intentional art-being* that a) delivers the charm, b) points to the possibility of re-considering the interaction and quiddity and import of objects in this space at this time.

•

We could move this entire setup in there, I formulate in my head, referring to the ensemble sitting current-ly at the *edge* of the gallery, occupying, fascinatingly enough, physically so, that liminal space where it is not *in, not part* of the work but actually constructing *the border*, acting *as* the divider, since there is no door, and no established space. The possibility that this set-up go 'in' there, *in the show*, is what is not acted upon, what remains pending, what creates the tension and forces the interrogations—and encourages the nudge, or I shall say the *potential nudge*: it might or might not occur, and the pending possibility is ever more enticing and exciting and suspenseful. A perceptual shift, then, a *nudge, an imposed/invited sign of rethinking and re-positioning*. What is perceived is: a) the strange—and in that strangeness, alienating from an artistic perspec-tive—presence and effect of this ensemble on the rest of the gallery's objects; b) the possible transformation of the specific space—the gallery, its surroundings and the building itself; c) the entire spectrum of operations that is at play in the realm in which they are found. I begin, of course, to think of elaborating the same phenomenon in different works, with different twists...

My own initial *perception of the potential nudge*, one that does not actually take place, is a pre-NothingDoing. It consisted in perceiving the potential realignment, which prompted a realignment to be fashioned. A pre-NoDo—with the *potential nudge* itself being the NothingDoing. This type of phenomenon though can get more and more complex, for it is of its very essence that it could be followed by a series of quick operations. Indeed, a next phase could develop (and the emphasis should be on the 'could'): the operation of actually transforming the physical space, whether by the first perceiver (I, in this case) or someone else. This next phase could constitute an actual physical gesture, one might say, since I or another person would be pushing, or re-placing, the ensemble 'into' the space, or redrawing the space, re-districting it, as it were, so that it actually *includes* the getup of the coffee machine and table with napkins etc., and changes it into an artwork. At this stage, the operations have gone beyond the NoDo one might say, especially if the doer is the perceiver. If the doer is *not* the perceiver (in this case, for example, I would be prompting someone else or encouraging someone else to go forth with the *actual* nudge), the perceiver could remain in the realm of the NoDo indeed, while the do-er has entered a realm of action through the suggestion of the NoDoist.

The NothingDoing/Nudge and the possibility of an extended nudge for everyone is all around us: the possibility of bringing *into the sphere of artworks objects or events or whatnots that lie at its periphery*—that, literally, construct the border with the terrain where the artworks are on display or in action. The Nudge liberates, and it does more: it transforms the world of art in a soft-protest kind of way. *The Nudge Revolution*, a 'violet' type of revolution, an insistent challenging of the borders and the lines (and the liens) that have been drawn (and placed).

The Nudge is also liberating for the seasoned NoDoist—constitutes, in fact, a path to becoming a seasoned NoDoist. The Nudge is freedom, and the personification of constant, fluid, evolutive transformation of the fields of art creation, and art display. The NothingDoing/Nudge: a fast, adaptable, mobile, effusive, uncatchable and unbreakable redistricting machine, redefining mechanism, and, again I say, liberating mantra. Interrogating inclusions and exclusions, fomenting discords and accusations, interrupting and intervening in the world. The Nudge is a quietly revolutionary way of being and operating. A fantastic tool in the NoDoist's toolkit.

·

7. Narra

I cannot say for certain why it was that the Boston bomb-ing is the one that led to the articulation of this NoDo—but it was there that it dawned upon me. Perhaps be-cause of the constantly shifting narratives, perhaps because of the *layers* of *simultaneous narrative con-struction*, the contradictory reports, along with the con-stant eaves-dropping and voyeurism that was at play. Perhaps because one got the sense that the entire she-bang was being concocted, created, *as it was unfolding*, with the reportage of the unfolding creative narrative as *part* of the very narrative. Not news then, so much as a an intricate *real-time narrative being scripted*, with cer-tain parts inflexible, while others were being fashioned depending on the circumstance without significantly af-fecting the overall structure or the main parts of the con-tent. Not a conspiracy theory, this, although we, admit-tedly, do not believe the official version. No matter what, the *sensation* that the events were unfolding according to a developing and invented narrative is indubitable—the details of that narrative being up for debate.

Thus, the narration of unfolding events was taking place: I had only to follow it, to be concocting, along with it. A participant in the creation *because* a voyeur, along with everyone else. That is the essence of the experience of such media in our age: real-time events, with the watchers as creators, not just passive participants. And, lest it be forgotten, there were many layers of watchers in the Boston bombings, being watched in turn, and contributing to the directions in which the narrative was going.

.

So many images have passed by before! So many images, so many narratives, so many tales and constructions—right before our eyes. Overwhelming our senses. And making protagonists of us all as well: tellers and told—we being, after all, in all of the other tales and all the other propaganda, all the other stories and tales and fabrications, all the narratives paraded nightly on the tube, somehow, manipulated, and, perhaps more, *manufactured*, as watching and listening entities, as actors on a strange stage. Narrated and narratees at once.

The shifting subtleties, the constant change of the nature of events as they unfold on television and in media around us further complicate our role. Who we are and what we are, and what narratives are born of this shifting identity, make for quite a bit of ambiguity and possibility when it comes to our agency in the formation of narratives. And thus the NothingDoing/Narra: as these supposedly new and unscripted events unfold, and the hyper and hysteric players on the tubes (TV, internet and coming variations) run amok and fashion the narratives and take us along for the rides, all one needs to do is *narrate exactly what was happening in the zones of the outer self, on television, online* or what have you. Narrate the narration even, and give way to the actual narration without edulcoration—without change: there, the affabulations will be revealed! The stories will happen! The novels will be written, because they are written already, or are being written as one recounts simply the event.

Here is where the NothingDoing comes. Since all one has to do is narrate the unfolding narratives without any type of intervention, there is actually no reason to record, make manifest, announce or otherwise make public the narrative we have concocted through the existing one. In other words, a grand NothingDoing is performed, whereby *the witnessed unfoldings are simply imagined as being re-narrated*, along with the various layers of the meta-narratives embedded in them—and that is all.

•

See the passersby even: they stand behind the anchorwoman and make faces as she, desperately serious, remains oblivious to their buffoonery. Others watching, others consoling, others reporting. Even on the endless repeats of the frames, and, of course, the *twists* in the narrative—and the *corrections* in the narrative, and the *twists within the corrections*! The point here, ladies and gents, is *not*—I repeat, *not*—to demonstrate how 'truth' is stranger than fiction, as the cliché goes; nor is it to fashion a new narrative technique; nor is it to unveil the ways in which propaganda rules our lives; not even to show how the spectacle is the very unfolding within which we participate. No, none of this is the point. The point is to recognize—and celebrate—*emergence*: the coming-to-the-surface of a new type of NothingDoing, a new species of NoDo born of one's sudden illumination, where *the actual narration*—which does *not* need to be in a loud voice or written or otherwise constructed— *the narration of the spectacle, I repeat, is concocted for us*, and, more importantly even, *the narration of the narration*, the narration of the unfolding is happening already. And thus, the NothingDoing: simply imagining yet not engaging in, the retelling, the redirecting, of the narration. *Simply narr-ing*. A copy, as close as can be, that is actually never undertaken.

O what a relief this NoDo is! At once reaffirming the propagandic nature of all the news and narratives coming our way, and simultaneously allowing these fables and farces to take their places among the af-fabulations—through the wondrously clever Nothing-Doing. Through which, I might add, propaganda, and the attempt at forcing down your throat certain tales, turns into what it should be: *the incredulous specta-cle of the farce*. The actual fashioning of this Nothing-Doing is *another form of resistance*—a clamoring un-heard, unseen and unmanifest, as I keep repeating, and certainly unannounced, but an art form neverthe-less. The NothingDoing/Narra allows sanity to remain, consciousness to retain some semblance of indepen-dence, perception to remain alert, cognition to remain sharp—and our being, our whole being, to remain alive still, somehow, alive... Still. A marvelous antidote, a fab-ulous *pièce de résistance*, a most necessary *weapon*, the NothingDoing/Narra is a type of NoDo that will be with us for long, perhaps as long as we live. And so be it. Indeed, so be it: we shall sing its praises and have recourse to it: yet another NoDo to save the day—yes, yet another to save us from our selves, and others...

•

8. Etina

(The Eternal Incomplete)

On a morning stroll with Plato Nubis (his real name—his parents had thought to combine the ethereal sugges-tion of clouds with the reasoned and rational image of Plato), along the banks of the river, we were sud-denly mesmerized by a group of three men working relentlessly, it seemed, on a boat docked in the harbor. I use 'the boat' as a direct object because neither I, nor he, knew exactly what aspect of the boat they were working on—or what the nature of the activity was: re-pair, enhancement, amelioration, or any combination thereof. We were not the only ones who had stopped. We were standing next to a couple who seemed to be visiting on an early morning stroll, a jogger who had also stopped—although, pausing momentarily, he kept jogging in place in that ridiculous manner of the driven and committed and undeterred athlete—and a young student, it seemed, who, pensive, walking along the wharf with a book under her arm, had even sat down to watch the decidedly unintentional show.

Have I ever told you of my Eternal Incomplete works, I asked Plato. (He and I often conversed about our literary and artistic projects, and, especially during our strolls, when we could expect to continue our conversations.) You have not, he responded with a smile. I pointed to the men working on the boat: a couple on the deck, another standing, miraculously it seemed, on the edge, and another, harnessed, strapped to the mast moving up and down. You see them: working away—or so we think—and not intending—again, so we think—for the passerby or the bathers or the curious strollers to stand and gaze—to watch, in effect, the show. I paused and that prompted him to utter a simple 'Go on!' after my silence (which seemed to have gone on more than one would expect).

Once upon a time, I continued, as I was on duty in the galleries of an eminent museum, I noticed that a crowd would form slowly—a large crowd, in fact—while the installers were installing works for the upcoming exhibition. There was nothing exceptional about the actual works that were being presented: not in terms of medium, not in terms of content, and not in terms of scale. Still, the presence of the installers, the climbing up and down of ladders, the movement to and fro of large pieces, the packaging, the placement, the displacement and replacement of works, all seemed to hold the attention of the museum-goers to an incredible degree. I can tell you that the phenomenon so fascinated me that I made a point to actually count the number of visitors in the adjacent galleries, where the works were already hanging, and also count the number of visitors that would linger. Considerably less, I found out, and the works in that adjacent gallery, where way fewer folks chose to hang around, were among the classics of our time, I must say. I also made a point, weeks later, to return to this very same gallery once the show had been finished and had been installed, only to be shocked not only at the comparatively low number who would bother to take in the show or even linger longer than a few seconds, but at the fact that the number of visitors here was significantly lower than the adjacent one that had had so few numbers compared to the 'Installation' if I may. I paused again, and this time, while we were both still gazing ahead at the workers on the boat, good old Plato Nubis, said: 'I think I know where you're going to go with this my man—and I must tell you, I really like it!'

•

I carried on with a smile—hoping that I would not let him down with his expectations now raised. I thought, I started again, that the most interesting aspect of that entire installation had been *the process of the instal-lation*—not the process of the creation of the works, in this case, but the process of installing works that the audience knew to be finished, or imagined finished. The differentiation is crucial: for, even though we know that audiences are fascinated with witnessing *processes* in general—and everything that happens *behind the scenes*—and specifically of the *creation of an artwork* (you need only look at any throng assembled around a sidewalk spray-painter), in this case, the expectations were of the process of installing work—a master work at that—assumed to have been finished. Thus, the *expectant fascination* was with the logic of the creation and composition of the *installing*—and I must use the term 'installing' as a noun for the very ironic reason that it must be differentiated from the term 'installation' which has indeed come to be a *type* of artwork. The fascination then, was with the logic of the ordering, as it were, with *how it will all look when complete*.

The next steps were easy, I told Plato, who was already onto my revelation: I set out to create such works where the *faux installating of an assumed finished work, in process, was the actual work*, except that in my case, 'works' that were not only not finished but that did not even exist. The *semblance of the installating*, the *process of an assumed installating* of the work, was the actual event, while the attraction of the unsuspecting audience was with the witnessing of

the process of the actual installing of an actual exhib-
it, which they had assumed without, I might add, any
false advertisement. The work, in effect, which went
on during the entirety of the exhibit, was *the unending
installating*. And once more, apologies are in order for
the awkward neologism that is *installating*, a gerund
I'm using as a noun (and verb in appropriate spots),
and that is a must in order to differentiate from the slew
of sibling terms, including 'installation' *and* 'installing'!

As Plato and I gazed in silence at the quiet, measured
and wondrously paced movements of the workers on
the boat, he said, laughing: 'And I assume you carried
on with this kind of charade in other locales, at other
times.' He had said this while keeping his eyes on the
sea and the boat, but then turned to me and smiled:
'The Eternal Incomplete, ey?' I did not have much to
add. Plato Nubis, a friend of the eternal kind, I must
say, knew of what he spoke.

I had one more detail to bring to Plato's attention, and
that was the actual differentiation of the NothingDoing
inspired by these observations, and the actual *doing*
of some of the *installatings*. You see, I commenced
again, I did indeed embark on actual *installatings* in a
number of locales, and always with a certain degree
of success, if I may say so. But my true find, my true
calling, lay in the fashioning of a NothingDoing that

was related to the *installatings*. And it was the ascension to the NothingDoing version that was much more proficient, and much more fabulous, in many ways truer to the idea than ever I could imagine, for it could happen much more often, without permits or partnerships, without actual audiences or visible processes of installing of any kind.

I had, indeed, for months and years thereafter, carried on the *installatings*, but soon after, for even more years, I had indeed fashioned the NothingDoing/Etina, in a host of locales and with a host of different parameters than the initial events in the gallery recounted. Where nothing was ever done, nothing ever finished or complete, nothing at all installed finally, or installated, or any process ended—or begun even. I might add that the nothing was in fact, just that: nothing at all. All was illusion: the poetic motions of faux workers in space nothing but a trance, in effect, a dance without beginning or end, the choreography of a majestic and balletic NothingDoing in motion. I was seeing the installatings and I was concocting installatings and potential installatings and taking to the extreme the original installatings: there was no need to have a faux work and the unending process of installating it with an unsuspecting audience. At the extreme, at its logical conclusion, we had arrived at the NothingDoing/Etina, where no installating was done, no process finished or begun.

Plato Nubis smiled again as we continued to gaze at the clouds and the sea and the boat and the workers, and even at the other strollers of this morn, then quickly turned and grabbed me by the elbow and intoned for us to carry on. 'The Etina,' he murmured as we turned and marched along the wharf, 'to that NoDo we must all aspire.' Yes, the NothingDoing/Etina: a glorious and unending work, a work that saves, a work that enchants, a work that makes one feel: alive!

·

9. Myto

(The Mighty Oak)

It was too long, I must admit, before I discovered that the most glorious of the NothingDoings might very well be constituted by the *turning into artworks* of all that *already exists in nature and all around*. And that renders all that one attempts to create most laughable when faced with all of these splendid creations. Lest I fall into an awful cliché, this is perhaps the most obvious, if not the most primitive, of NothingDoings as well, one which consists of fashioning the condition for things and phenomena—whether unfolding in time or not, of varieties of hues and colors and shapes, of different scales—to be *revealed as artwork* precisely by *the creating of the conditions for this perception*, by the fashioning of a relationship with these things and phenomena that are made to be seen and signified *as* artworks, legitimate artworks that is, with the literal use of the term artwork (and not a metaphoric or otherwise figurative use of it). Thus, the repositioning of the *relationship* of the experiencer of outwardly phenomena:

a *recalibration of the modality of perception and cognition*, and thus a recalibration of the necessity of 'doing' anything, along with a recalibration of the categories.

•

I speak here of the movement of the glaciers along the waters in the north. I speak here of an abstract painting born of the variations in hue and seemingly fervent gestures made upon a surface by unintentional actors. I speak here of the bicyclist's ride on the road where he piercingly makes out the swiftly passing grainy dots on the asphalt of the pavement. I speak here of the formation of rocks along the wharf on a Caribbean isle. Or even of the movement of the crabs along these rocks on the same wharfs. And, again, I must insist, I speak not of them as: a) metaphoric or figurative masterworks that we are dubbing artwork to give them a certain value, or a certain quiddity; b) subjects of artworks (like photographs or paintings, say); c) entities or phenomena that turn into artwork upon their capture, upon their 'graphing' in a recognized artistic field. No, I speak of them as artworks in waiting, in essence, *transformed literally into artworks through the NothingDoingal poetics.*

These are not artworks per se, or rather, in and of themselves—that is where the cliché would lie—but are *rendered into artworks* by the *reveal* that occurs through the fashioning of the conditions by the perceiver, the experiencer, the liver of life. That is precisely what renders one *alive*, renders one a *liver* : that is what makes life, for these conditions to be fashioned. One must thus *actively engage in the cultivation of a NothingDoing* in order to perceive, experience, live, the 'art' that is thus fashioned. And if we were to quarrel about the definition of artwork, I refer the reader to other parts of this document where my own theoretical affinities are revealed.

This erasure of all activity, the lack of intervention, the lack of communication even, these fashionings of conditions is perhaps one of the most difficult of endeavors, for it is also the active cultivation of a certain *brand of silence*, the active cultivation of a certain *dispersion of thought*, a *deliberate pushing away of ideas* even—even the great ones. And I dare say that this brand of silence, this dispersive and pushing away are *not* easily associated with similar cultivation in other practices—yoga, for example, or meditation—or even strong concentration. No, these are unique, singular and most notorious to achieve. They are *particular to the NothingDoings*, particular it must be said, to them all, but in this specific case too, particular to this subtype of NothingDoing, to this, this particular type of NothingDoing, the NothingDoing/Myto—inspired, the name, by such a construct long ago as we engaged with a mighty oak.

•

I see, still, the glacier moving, I see, in the mountains, the light falling upon the window, I see the ruins of a ghost-town, unbearable and poetic... But it was a mighty oak, the great tree, upon which my gaze one day was resting that taught me, that revealed to me, the possibility of birthing this new type of NothingDoing. I could not even begin to describe the ecstasy that I lived in those moments when the mighty oak and I were united, nor can I do justice to the sensations that I lived as I was constructing the NothingDoing/Myto. Let it be said that I promised, to myself and that Mighty Oak (yes, capital letters now), that the revelation of the possibility of the NothingDoing, and the actual unfolding of the NothingDoing, were enough for me to bestow a slightly transformed name in honor of that Mighty Oak upon the entire *type* of NothingDoing that had been revealed. The *Myto*, then, became, in honor of that beloved Mighty Oak, the name of the subspecies of NothingDoing that had to do with the *reveal* of the artness of existing phenomena. What higher honor could one bestow, I cannot be sure...

O Mighty Oak, how we shall place you in the museum

one day we shall, and have the opening, with everyone around you silently watching, O Mighty Oak, the greatest ever art show in the history of mankind... Except that they probably won't—but still we did it: through you, we gave the world a new type of NothingDoing, an eminently glorious NothingDoing, the mighty Myto—yes, the NothingDoing/Myto!

•

III

The following is an exchange that is said to be among the most revealing in <u>The Book of NoDo</u> (Legends of the Textings, 42.2). In it, a pilgrim queries the Guide, who promptly responds, and, soon, learns of the possessions of the pilgrim, upon which he scolds him and tells him basically to get on with it, and yet simultaneously warns him to heed the tricks of the evil-doers...
An enigma and a riddle, both rolled into each other, if there ever were two...

The Guide writes (in a text): 'The path to NoDohood is long and treacherous. You must cross many rivers and climb many mountains. It is infinitely more difficult to NoDo than to Do. This is your phrase of the day, every day. After you have sweated out your jobs with a run or a visit to the gym or the yoga studio, you will sit in front of Television, open Beer Can (or Bottle), a bag of Chips, and stare ahead. You will then ask yourself: why do I DO all that. And you will see where you go. We will hold a seminar to discuss your findings tomorrow.'

The pilgrim reveals that he has no TV. No beer. 'Forgive my insolence most masterful maestro of NoDo,' he is said to have texted, 'but could I substitute bourbon, popcorn and computer? Or is computer too do-orific? Popcorn too much of an accomplishment (stovetop pcorn, i have no microwave?!)! This is hard.'

The Guide writes: 'Ah!! Pilgrim on the Path!! You speak of wanting to take the journey to becoming a practitioner of NoDos, and yet you reveal to me that you possess no TV and no microwave oven!! And that your popcorn will pop in the oven!! This is simply impermissible!!! Can you imagine venerable ninja warriors without swords? Football players without helmets? This is troublesome. You must write a thesis on how you plan to overcome this. It will be challenging. But not impossible. This may be your first challenge as a NoDoist. We will then assess your ideas with the help of advanced rubrics. Do this tonight. You must. Do this. (Beware The Edict, for you never know the tricks of the doers, of whatmore they are up to!)'

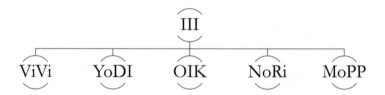

10. ViVi

(The Viewer on View)

Now the NothingDoing/ViVi: the persistent, consistent, pertinacious artwork that consists of deploying all senses to understand *the phenomenon of the ViVi—the Viewer on View*. This is a NoDo that is founded upon, and thrives on, *operations upon another artwork*: invisible operations, unarticulated operations, unexpressed operations, upon an artwork. This is a NoDo that reveals the actual status of a certain *other* piece: a NothingDoing that consists in *deciphering and deconstructing our experience vis-à-vis an artwork*—the one that actually has constructed a dormant 'viewer on view' phenomenon at play. A NothingDoing that is put into motion *through the existence of a previously categorized artwork*.

Valiantly, and quite riskily I must say, I speak not only of those works where the ViVi phenomenon is obvious—we can cite, easily, among the grand works in the canons, Picasso's *Demoiselles d'Avignon*—where the experience leads one to become aware of one's own gaze, seeing oneself literally being on view. Not even, for example, Seurat's pointillism, which ultimately places one in the situation of becoming cognizant of how we are forming images—constructing images—how we are *seeing*, thus coming to see our own position as viewers. No, I speak of all situations when one is confronted with the subtle gestures, the layered works, the works of the less well-known practitioners of the subtle ViVi—that is, any true artist!

The NothingDoing/ViVi is something akin to *a meditative verification*—a secret operation that verifies or debunks the degree to which a categorized artwork actually puts into motion the phenomenon of sensing oneself on view. To what degree it makes that phenomenon *known* to the experiencer of the piece (the viewer, in the case of 'visual' artworks). Perhaps the most controversial of the NoDos, were it not for the fact that no one actually will know of the operation. And, of course, the NoDo/ViVi can go across the various landscapes— geographical, physical, emotional, mental—to see, to dig, to appreciate, to recognize, all the artworks that surround us.

Ah, I can see the reader protesting, 'Did you not say it is a NoDo occurring around categorized artworks?' And I: I did—but I lied. This meditative NoDo occurs all around, always to detect, and protect, as art, all the ViVi phenomena that surround us—and not only that, but various iterations of the phenomena. *That* is the glory of the NothingDoing/ViVi as well: the regeneration of the gaze, the meta-gaze: the story of Art (with a capital A) without works thus labeled.

The story of the NoDo/Vivi is a short and subtle tale of reflections upon the gaze. A deceptive one it is, *resting on the ruins of the gazes*—the gazes all: the only artwork possible when faced with other art, or the stuff of the world that generates the ViVi phenomenon. One that can accompany one on all ventures. One that allows one to create art when faced with art, and when not. A provocative machine that allows a certain type of engagement. Always. An artwork resting on the experiencing of a cognition of the metagaze. That is the strength and the subtle power of the NoDo/Vivi—an eternal companion. An eternally loyal companion. An eternally wondrous companion.

•

11. YoDI

(You Do It)

I took aside Jasquonax Saydi-Sax the other day and told him of the idea of constructing a quote unquote sculpture in the middle of the park that would disintegrate soon after. I'll help you with it, he said. And then, pleased that he had offered, I said, 'No, you do it.'

'I do it?' he responds, puzzled.
'Yes you do it, all yours, you go ahead and do it.'
'I'll be your assistant,' he says.
'Assistant shmassistant,' I say. 'You do it, it's yours.'
'Mine how,' he says, stunned, and getting slightly irritated.
'Yours yours,' I say. 'No secret and no ambiguity. You do it, you sign it: your work.'

•

Expectedly, the response is along the lines of *ownership* and *copyright*—legal and moral, in effect. 'But you came up with it,' he says. 'Who cares,' I say. We then get into a whole discussion about the millennial-old and arguably controversial practices of apprentice-ship and appropriation in all directions, including a discussion of those artists whose ideas are incorporated and owned by them, with the actual works constructed or fabricated by their assistants or teams. 'The other thrust in this type of construction,' he says, 'is to equate your work with that of the conceptual or co-conceptual artists. Your conception, my doing. What you're telling me,' he says thinking, 'is you don't care about the second, that is, the conceptual folks, and you're eschewing the first—the master/apprentice relationship.'

'Not just eschewing it,' I say. 'And besides, you are simplifying things.'

'That's right,' he says. 'Not *just*: you're saying it's yours—and thus, reversing, in effect, the first. Not just signing it and passing it, but *de-signing yourself*—and I sign it. Good old-fashioned generous gift: you're giving it to me!'

'That's one way to put it,' I tell him. 'But I do have something up my sleeve—not just for you, this!'

'I figured,' he smiles. 'Do tell!'

Well, you know about my NothingDoings right, I've been telling you about them more or less? 'Yes,' he says, 'more or less. Less, I'd say, but yes.' Well, I explain, my actual *giving* to you of the work that you will reconstruct or make or fabricate, however you want to say it, and that you will ultimately, through the process of making, conceptually transform, this work that you'll make is *yours*. 'Go on,' he says, after a slight pause on my part. In my case, I say, I *did not do nothing*, I actually *did a NothingDoing*. He smiles. 'Come again my man,' he says. 'Please, come again.' The invitation to you to actually do it, I continue, my giving the concept of a work but not doing anything, that is, the conceptualizing of it and the extension of it to someone else who will actually do it, the *auto-appropriation-allowance*, constitutes, on my part, a NothingDoing, a particular type of NothingDoing, one I dub the YoDI, for *You Do It*: a situation where I don't actually do anything but sequence these operations together—which leads to the work. I'm giving you the work. Not nothing.

•

'I see,' Saydi-Sax says. 'Your work is the getting-and-passing and mine can be re-conceptualizing or not, and fabricating, or not.' Kind of, I say, but not quite. There is no need to rename, to rebrand. It is a new type of art form, the NothingDoing, and the YoDI is a subtype of the NothingDoing. See it for what it is, and it makes perfect sense. We both laughed at the enunciation of the last four words. Maybe not perfect, but it makes good sense, I smiled. And yes, the master/apprentice relationship, and the ideal of the conceptual artist passing on the fabrication to a worker are similar practices, *neighborly* practices, but they are *not the same*. Call it what it is, think of it how it should be, and you will be fine, I repeated. No need for comparison or approximation with what you already know. Take the time, rather, I expounded (even though I could see the annoyance in him rising as I tended towards more lecturing), take the time to understand the subtleties of the YoDI for themselves, and you will be fine.

His retort was expected and his grasp of the potential of the YoDI swifter than I would have anticipated. 'And I,' says he, 'could I swing it back to you, or onto another?' I smiled a knowing smile: the *extended YoDI chain*, I said, or even the *eternal YoDI chain*, the essence of the life of NothingDoing personified! Bravo, I exclaimed after that quick answer. Bravo indeed.

The YoDI has the potential to be an eternal work, an *unending work*, a *perpetual work*, like no other before it. 'I dare say, perhaps it has already occurred,' he says, 'and many a time!' With that, I disagreed. It has not, I insisted, for it has not been branded thus. Or conceived thus. But now, it has. It has launched, and could quite easily be perpetuated forever. Only as a NothingDoing though. Only as that. The grand NothingDoing/YoDI. Now it can go on forever.

12. OIK

(Only I Know)

This type of NothingDoing is founded on the provoca-tion of work by others—work that by definition could only be begun and finished by others—except for the launching phase. The first of such works was revealed to me as the phrase 'Only I Know' came to mind. It was a very particular situation that I am hesitant to share, but where you must trust that what was initiated was indeed the completion of a piece by others, without anyone really knowing that they were involved in any type of what I would call artwork, a NothingDoing, specifically. It is, decidedly, not about incompleteness, which many other NoDos proudly put into motion.

Still true to its non-manifest and unannounced at-tributes, the NothingDoing/OIK is a fine example of 'provocation without recognition' that the NothingDo-ing can incite. The artists, the provocatees, are not only not aware that *they themselves are creating a work of art*, but they are also oblivious to the fact that *the incitation, the prompt—rather, the process and ritu-al, the trick, yes, the trick of fomenting their artwork—is itself part of an artwork*, a NoDo/OIK. This particular it-eration of the NoDo is thus named after one of its most iconic iterations—the phrase 'Only I Know'—much in the way the 'cadavre exquis' begins to refer to a *type* of drawing, a method, when really the name was con-cocted after one of the first and most iconic images was the result of that process at the beginning of the experimentations.

The work, then, the NothingDoing/OIK consists of the initiation of a question or a phrase that prompts others into completing the work. Initiating the kinds of phras-es, the kinds of expressions that can only be com-pleted by others. Not quite a participatory work, not exchange practices, no, but a work that relies on the initiatives and incompletions: an overture, in effect, let-ting people 'run' with it, complete it, whether they want to share or not. This type of work in due time prompts *listening*, the very essence of *taking a back seat*, the creation of the condition of crumbling, or retreat—*yes, retreat: a lamenting and a retreat.*

·

A next step of this NothingDoing, an iteration of this NoDo, would surely lie in *prompting others to actu-*

ally come up with the prompt, and soon enough, *prompting others to actually prompt others to come up with the prompt*, rather than come with the prompt oneself—an eternal chain, then, that carries on. The criteria of such a chain could be illustrated by the exemplary *Only I Know*. Imagine the rest of this: an endless phrase leading to a secret, a mystery unveiled, a confession, a novel perhaps, or some other grand elaboration. In any of these cases, the progenitor of the phrase by definition could not claim to be able to continue the prompt, let alone pretend to do it in an 'interesting' way. It is *the prompting of the construction of other works*: a *prompting* that must remain without manifestation and remain unannounced at that. A sudden burst and a quick goodbye, all while the 'other' knows not that both dimensions were artworks (their invention and the prompting).

Could one argue that the NoDo/OIK is in effect a *faux* NothingDoing, an approximate one, since there is clearly the occurrence of the phrase, the manifestation of the phrase—whereby a very concrete phrase is concocted and birthed into the world? Not quite, for although there is a manifest phrase, the NoDo is not the actual uttering of the phrase, but the initiation of the chain, the invisible, unannounced and definitely not-manifest *carrying on* of the perpetuated chain. We may even continue this elaboration and recognize that this itinerary, this overture need not be a linguistic phrase, but could, indeed, be any other type of construct, that also provokes the same type of phenomenon: a launch and a recoiling—a launch, I repeat, of something that by definition needs to be done by others. Not an incomplete work, not a participatory work. One could say a cumulative work if one wishes, but that is not even the intent—for the results do not need to be gathered, need not be accumulated, need not be brought together, need not be grouped to make a whole.

The result, ultimately, is unknown—since the work *derived* from the NoDo can take any shape. (And the bringing together of those works is decidedly not a NoDo, whatever it turns out to be.) The work—the NothingDoing/OIK—is the launching of the overture: the conceptualizing of the overture, and the launching, yes, through a mysterious mechanism. That is the OIK: the bringing of wondrousness into the world...

·

13. NoRi

(No Redirect Necessary)

'I am so tired,' once upon a time a friend said, 'that they can pick the pieces of me off the floor anytime!' These were the exclamations! Such exclamations constituted nuggets that one could *pick,* pick like a flower, and *redirect* into an œuvre. Redirect into an ongoing body of work. Redirect into a literary or artistic piece, as they say. This is what I used to do! The habit and passion of the writer: circulate, notate, redirect. It always meant listening, seeing, seeking—and taking seriously the utterances. Children, adults, the down-and-outs, anyone really. There are groups among us who are constantly combining words and ideas and images in fascinating ways, given their age, their professions, their mental condition or their cognitive abilities. Utterances that could be 'literary' if only they knew how to redirect them into a body of work. Well, I always thought, it was my duty to collect and redirect. The ways in which various people expressed themselves were full of tropes and figures, metaphors and analogies and many more wondrous and original, if not intentional, manipulations of language, that one would have a very difficult time concocting or inventing out of the blue. Their imaginations were not at play, but their modes of expressions, perhaps because of a lack of knowledge of the language even, would lead to certain associations that were full of charm and revelation. Perhaps they are missing the actual correct expression and thus assembling words and images that turn out to be quite powerful and suggestive. Perhaps they are juxtaposing elements that usually would not go together, unaware that that actually became a method in one of the more impactful art movements of the previous century. Perhaps they are hesitating and bifurcating and concocting and bringing into the fold images that we have eschewed. Again, whatever the *mechanisms* that prompt the inevitable *lines or words or sentences*, whatever the sources and reasons for these, entire groups or particular individuals, in all areas of life, in all corners of all daily lives, *come up with stuff:* nuggets of wisdom, great lines, great expressions, great *tropological figures*, whose truth-value is undeniable, and where form and content are intricately linked.

But there was something more. The actual engagement on my part—the constant listening, seeing, circulating and collecting, picking (as in *cueillir*, I am really tempted to say)—allowed me to actually survive the world! All was material to me, I used to say, *all is material to me*. And the pun notwithstanding, it meant that all the stuff of the world could be turned into material for an œuvre, a piece, a work—and through that mechanism, the ways of the world became bearable: the incoherence, the chaos, the madness, all became bearable, because it *could be turned into material for literature*. And it saved me: time and time again, the *redirect* into an art piece, into a literary piece especially, saved me.

•

Now, this has for long been a method of creation, as I said, when the assumption was that the work involved *doing something* with these *finds*. In fact, it constituted a method, for yours truly and surely for others. It consisted of putting into motion manners of finding the most in terms of quantity, finding the best, in terms of quality, but certainly it also included being consistently aware of the potential of these occurrences, to find those places and circumstances where things could happen and I could note them, 'record' them, in effect, and turn them into something! Oh, how my works bear the traces of this for the discerning reader! How the characters, how the language... And those works that I admire too: you see and feel how the author noted the nuggets and fragments and either integrated them as

such, or in slightly transformed ways. All across litera-
ture and all across art, you see the picking of material,
the *redirection* into an œuvre.

Well... The next step—and if not *next step*, then an *alter-
native*, which retains the potential to continually save
me, as I have said this ritual and operation and habit
does—is to *forego the actual redirection*, perhaps to
imagine or even entertain the thought, but not actual-
ly do it. Enter thus another type of NothingDoing, the
NothingDoing/NoRi. What the NoRi does in this case,
is to liberate the scriptor, the writer, the artist, liberate
them from the steps that follow the actual picking, the
steps after the wondrous finds are obliterated, and the
finds turned into a new type of NoDo—that is, the no-
tation is eliminated, the re-direction is eliminated, and
the *sculpting* of the find into the fabric of the work is
ignored as well. The sculpting, as it were, is made at
the level of the NothingDoing.

The world is *still* material. The integration does occur.
The relationship of the writer/artist to the stuff of the
world also remains—in fact, may even go deeper as
one fully *penetrates* the material that will not be re-
directed anymore. For, knowing that one will actually
forego the redirection into an actual work, the turning
of the stuff into potential material in the mind, the pick-
ing of fragments as sure-fire material that will never-

theless *not* find a home in any single piece or work, has the potential to be that much deeper, that much more appreciated at that stage of the picking and consideration as material, a stage that will now be the last, instead of a way to something else.

•

The find, then, the fragment, remains a type of material. One must not make the mistake of thinking that 'no redirect' signifies a mere recognition of the potential of that fragment for a heretofore uncreated piece. It's not that the cognition of a phrase or an image or an expression is *just appreciated*, it is not that it is just followed by a smile and the knowledge that one could have 'picked' or 'planted' it—no, it is *fashioned into a NothingDoing*. We had, truth be told, hesitated in dubbing this NoDo a *No Redirect*, but the lack of the regular redirect, that is, the lack of an operation that turns those fragments into a piece or a work, should not throw us off. The lack of a redirect into an œuvre, constitutes the fashioning of the NoDo. One is tempted to say that it is a redirect into a NoDo, but, again, that would be incorrect: *the lack of a redirect into a piece allows the NothingDoing to come into being: that is the work—and that is the path*.

One could say, in fact, that in an advanced stage of

consciousness for the artist and certainly for the No-Doist, this type of operating saves one even more, saves one even better, than the redirect into material for the œuvre. All is a NoDo to me, should be the new, personal, and certainly impossible-to-grasp euphemism. Hail the NoDo/NoRi, for all is a NoDo to me...

•

14. MoPP

(Moving Past Projects)

Under the tree in the park across from the small flat in which we live, one morning, at dawn, a conversation with Xerzac Elivayno who had come from out of town and was planning to stay a couple of days, launched us into an exploration of one of my personal favorite NoDos. His queries and arguments had to do with the relevance of any work that was currently being done by playwrights, by poets, by the prose stylists, and by others still, including the scholars, along with all the construction and makings of the sculptors, the paint-ers, and even the filmmakers and other interdiscipli-narians. His query arose out of the despair he was encountering with any of the works and his lack of conviction of the necessity to really, as he said, par-ticipate at all. 'Would the world not be better off,' he asked, 'if I did *not* contribute?!' I smiled and nodded approvingly. Listen, I said, I certainly can't tell you that it would be best if you did not participate, but I must say, I know where you are coming from. Too many people make things. Too many create, one could say, and there's just lots and lots of things and stuff out there—no matter how you look at it—independently of the quality. I made a dramatic pause and turned to look at him directly—we both were gazing directly ahead as we spoke before that. Now, I must admit that I am quite cognizant of what you are talking about. And, in fact, have concocted a type of work that addresses this straight on. He, in turn, makes a dramatic gesture and turns and says: 'How so?'

Glad you asked, I smiled. The secret lies in the cultivation of a particular practice, one I've dubbed a NothingDoing—or NoDo, for short. He laughed and responded in a one-word response I quite appreciated: 'Brilliant!' He said, adding, almost immediately but with a pause of the thinker in-between: 'Absolutely brilliant!' And let me add, I continued without much of a pause, this is quite important as you can imagine, this is beyond the paradigm of presenting other types of objects, and beyond any declarative stoppage of work too—of which there have been plenty of examples of various kinds in the history of art. Quite the contrary: a higher ideal that we seek, a new universe. Here, the NothingDoing is a *type of artwork*, contesting the space and contesting the capitalistic and commercial thrust in everything. And, beware, I am not speaking of the 'art' of doing nothing, I am speaking of the No-

Dos—a glorious and salvific realm.

·

Xerzac was quite taken with these quick words about the NoDos, but retained one major, *major*, one must repeat, point of anxiety. What about the projects—what about the many projects one always has *en route*? That is, all the parts of projects that occupy one's mind, all the projects that have certain manifestations in early drafts? What does one do with all of those?! Yes, I acquiesced, depending on *when* one becomes conscious of the NothingDoing artworks and one's engagement in fashioning them, one could be paralyzed by the actions that need to be taken with and for the *already in process* projects, the already *en route* projects, as he called them. I added, though, that there was nothing to worry about, and that I'd tell him why. I paused, took a sip from the drink I had in my hand and even leaned back and looked up at the wondrous foliage of the trees.

First, I let out, still leaning back and speaking without looking at him directly, the NothingDoing is an actual artwork, which means, like any type of artwork and art form in which you are engaged, nothing holds you back from *simultaneously engaging in another form*. In other words, I told him, you can be engaged in

NothingDoings and *also* your other projects. I leaned back up and saw him nodding softly as if somehow relieved. You see what I'm saying, right? I added. To which he responded, out loud: 'Absolutely!' That's not all though, I said, there is more: something that might be even more useful and astonishing, and that relates to a NoDo that actually confronts head-on all those projects that you are speaking of. It is called Moving Past Projects, or the MoPP, more accurately the NothingDoing/Mopp. Xerzac Elivayno laughed and instructed me in no uncertain terms to continue, which I was all too willing to do.

The MoPP, I said, embraces the necessity of someone who is so ensconced in the NothingDoing way of life that they find it close to impossible to engage in any other type of artwork, to engage in the very specific NoDo that the MoPP is, the NothingDoing/MoPP. It is a NothingDoing that consists in *refashioning an existing project without any visible, manifest, or announced manner into a work that bears those same characteristics: unmanifest and unannounced*, and to actually *finish* them, *in that manner*. Imagine a *machine*, I told him, nowhere visible or manifest, that allows you to take all these *en route* projects you speak of, at any stage, whether you've just got a conceptualized seed or a grain of the potential project, or you are deep into it and simply don't know how to end or finish it, or you do even but don't want to take the time or make the effort to 'finish', and grinds them into oblivion—that is, not a 'finished' project, but into a project that is no more, at any stage of anything. Finished, you could also argue (and not, not-finished), but in this very particular and peculiar way! It is done, not existing, not a preoccupation, not anything that lingers or needs to be thought through. This, I told him, this NoDo/MoPP, remains an alternative for any practitioner of the NothingDoings, for all those who do not want to do a NoDo concurrently with any type of artwork—or those who find it impossible. And that machine, the actual NothingDoing that is the MoPP, that, my friend, is not manifest, and not announced, if you see what I'm saying.

•

Xerzac Elivayno continued to smile and nod. His smile was an acknowledgment of what he always thought of my own clever devilish tactics. I knew he would have something up his sleeve though and he did not disappoint. He said: 'Okay, let me now propose this to you—and I'm sure you have thought about it—but let me say-slash-ask you this. You are, in effect, creating the perfect salvation when it comes to artworks and art forms for anyone who has acceded to any type of engagement with the NothingDoings. For one, you are saying, you can continue with your other projects, and this does not diminish or taint your NothingDo-ings in any way. Correct?' Correct, I said. 'And for another,' he picked up, anticipating correctly that my response would be short and in accord with his con-clusion, 'you are saying that another *type of Nothing-Doing, the MoPP*, can also allow you to, and here the verb is missing, allow you to 'deal with' or 'get rid of' or 'bring to a conclusion' or 'finish' or whatever, all your other projects. And since it's a NoDo itself, you are fully engaged, not to mention enthralled, with the NothingDoing.' He paused, considered, and then ex-claimed: 'Correct?!'

•

I looked at Xerzac Elivayno under the tree that day after this one-word query and stayed silent a few mo-ments that surely seemed like an eternity. For I knew, and he did too, that a particular answer to that query could be the great salvation of all artists and writers and poets and scholars everywhere, the very people he had queried me about at the beginning of the con-versation. The great salvation of anyone who would have taken on the art forms known as the Nothing-Doings and who, over a good amount of time, would have mastered the many nuances and foundations and skills and competencies attached to the artwork. And since we also knew that many would never know

of the NothingDoings or perhaps not take them se-
riously when they did hear, or misinterpret or misun-
derstand or simply dismiss them, we also recognized
that it would be a loss to many and too bad, really,
for them... For we knew, again, that with my expect-
ed answer to his query, all was potentially solved, all
anxieties surrounding artworks and projects were
potentially solved, and maybe forever! A world of se-
renity and lucidity and wisdom awaited all those who
would thus be engaged in the NothingDoings, again,
depending on my answer. A great world, potentially, a
more wondrous world that anyone had ever known,
and more peaceful and paradisiacal than all images
and concepts of heavens and beheshts put together
in the stories and myths and legends of cultures an-
cient or modern!

Xerzac Elivayno awaited my response and in those
moments, the two of us knew that we had the fate of
all in our hands. I smiled at him—again, only a few mo-
ments had passed that seemed like eternities, where
time and all movements and sounds and everything
else had stopped—almost nodded and paused again,
suddenly, in my tracks. I smiled and exclaimed in no
uncertain terms: 'Correct!!'

Correct, I repeated, correct, my friend, correct indeed!
And then after calming down slightly, I even expound-

ed on the future language we could use in relation to this NoDo. The verb related to this NoDo, I whispered, can be 'to mopp', its gerund, 'mopping', and its past, 'mopped'—and all can be used in the appropriate circumstances. Use to your heart's delight! And that will be the salvation, I ended, Xerzac now beaming with an otherworldly smile, the invention of this language can save us all, thanks to the great NoDo, the NoDo/MoPP!

·

IV

—Doing nothing right this minute. Very different from a NothingDoing by the way...
—I'm not doing something. While some are doing knotting.
—Nodo guru approves of your commitment to not doing something. Doing knotting a bit different. Must have conversation with outlaw doing-knottingers... Those naughty knottingers...

O NoDos, thanks for at least granting me reprieves in these seas of doings.
Once I'm done with you O NoDos,
I can just refer to you in these moments,
not anymore 'work on' you.
Come soon O day of NoDos
in little redorgreenorcyan or some other color booklet in hand, or living on some cloud or in e-format.
Come soon.
For soon is not soon enough,
when it comes to you,
O NoDos...

From <u>The Book of NoDo</u>
(Legends of the Textings, 1.8)

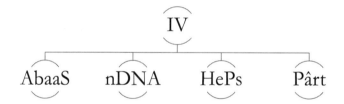

15. AbaaS

(Abandonment and Spectacle)

I gathered the followers and the non-followers and all those who once upon a time had left their paths and told them how glorious their journeys had been and I told them of abandonment. You are the true achievers I bellowed, and they all around began to clap and swoon and they knew that they in their abandonment and they in their non-attachment had been the highest achievers. They began to weep and they began to clap louder and weep still and then, upon my request, my arms up and back down to ask them for silence, they fell silent and in their silence the incitation for me to carry on.

This abandonment, my friends, I bellowed like a preacher or a millennial prophet, this abandonment is not only *part* of the œuvre and the new direction on a righteous path, but I'm here to tell you that this abandonment is another among the great artworks of our age, another in the species of that most glorious of offerings, that most enlightened of works, that most innovative concoction where form, style, structure, co-habit the same and great space and fashion the great artwork: the NothingDoing! That paragon of the embodiment of abandonment, the willful, powerful, abandonment: the glorious NothingDoing! Yes, I bellowed again, your abandonment is not only a great act and an advanced mode of behavior based upon enlightened consciousness, but it is also an *artwork* in and of itself—belonging to the now legendary family known as the NothingDoings!

·

Around me I sensed the great anticipation and appreciation for the new path: the newest of itineraries in the grand journey of the creation of artworks. A collective cry for embracing the new path went up. And almost immediately, the echoes rose from across the landscape we occupied: the fervor of abandonment, the fervor of the embrace of the NothingDoing/AbaaS.

Abandonment, my friends, I shouted in an almost trance, abandonment is the path to glory! Abandonment is the new great artwork! No more ambitions that rely on adopted frameworks! No more attempts at belonging! No more attachments! To objects, to concepts, to desires either! To experiences or to aesthetic principles! To projects or to works! To concepts such as finishing or completing! No attachments to the concept of abandonment even, I thundered, while all around and in a voluptuous and intoxicating crescendo, the crowd roared its approval. No attachment to the NothingDoing even, I laughed! It is entirely possible indeed, that you end up abandoning abandonment, for the lack of attachment that you have to it!

And they roared again and I in the midst of the call for abandonment and the further cultivating of the grand work, espoused the virtues—the glorious virtues—of the NothingDoing. And warned, simultaneously, of the insurgency of the sudden or the unexpected abandonment, one that could undermine itself, and the entire NoDo family as it were. I worried that the complexity and the paradox might befuddle the masses assembled but I was selling them short. They grasped it, they embraced it, they began chanting even, swaying and chanting and making up new slogans and new ditties and a new anthem even:

> *Hail to the NoDos and the abandonments*
> *Happy the freethinkers embracing abandonment*
> *Hail hail paradoxes and conundrums*
> *Happy the pilgrims of abandonment!*

Not the most poetic, but it mattered not! It was the

rhythm of the moment, the swaying itself, the longing and chanting, the embraces, the capting of the possibilities, the liberation at hand: the eternal liberation, the endless liberation, the victorious chant for AbaaS.

•

We have come a long way, I thundered again, wanting to bring to a close the day's events, and knowing that the audience would potentially tire of the extended ritual, and knowing also that they could not at present, in the rapturous trance they found themselves in, could not hear or grasp the rational, theoretical connection of the grand category and spectacle of the Nothing-Doing to that of abandonment. It was time to bring the session to a close, at least where I was concerned, and leave them to make the connections.

The simple edicts, along with the calls and the chants, were sufficient, when it came to this NothingDoing: to know that the spectacle of abandonment was the grandest of them all, this had been grasped—internalized, enlivened, forever a part of their beings. The abandonment and the spectacle. AbaaS: one of the glorious summits of the NothingDoing. The Nothing-Doing/AbaaS: the glorious apex of art.

•

16. nDNA

(The New Doing Nothing as Art)

They were assembled again the pilgrims, and to the assembled in the room I clamored and said in a passionate voice: I have no doubt that *the art of the NothingDoing*—I am speaking here of the artworks labeled NothingDoing, with all their subspecies—will be confused with that other fabulous practice, that marvelous terrain of bliss, that fantastic realm of otherworldly activity and inactivity, *the art of doing nothing*. Notice, I said, the placement (and not) of the various capital letters—even though they could not of course, since they were only listening.

The NothingDoing that, as I have previously clarified, can and should be classified as artwork, has subtle, nuanced and seriously differentiated meanings and connotations relative to the art of doing nothing. It is a mistake to equate the NothingDoing, the art form, with the art of doing nothing, I insisted—almost as if I had no trust in the perceiving of the difference. And perhaps one of the most consequential elements here is to recognize that being engaged in the fashioning of a NoDo is *not doing nothing*, and further, not doing anything should not be confused with the very rigorous, subtle and nuanced works that fall under the NothingDoings.

I paused, allowed the gathered to internalize and chew on my pronouncements. And let not the fools and the doubters and the mockers get the best of you, I cried. They are weary of frauds, and we cannot blame them. But you are not frauds, my brethren, and you certainly are not lazy and certainly not without skill. You have chosen to engage in the NothingDoings! And for that you must hold your head high, and keep your egos in check, and simply counter the doubts of the doubters and gently try to persuade them and explain to them the new art form. You must constantly remind them of the differences between the artists of the NothingDoings and the practitioners of the art of doing nothing, who are numerous indeed, and perhaps at a higher level of consciousness than all of us combined, and certainly all around us, for sure. Do not disparage, and do not be defensive: explain and carry on—and know that if you are taken for one who does nothing, perhaps it is in your best interest to thus be imagined after all!

.

And I carried on, now deeply in the throes of my an-
nouncements. Be not alarmed, I cried, for I, even, attri-
bute my inability to completely abandon the Nothing-
Doings and reach contentment within the art of doing
nothing to a strange attachment to doing something—
or categorizing all things done and not, as art. And that
attachment, I sense, must have some sort of strange
relation to a psychological and emotional make-up, a
temperament, a being-in-the-world that I am not cur-
rently willing—and frankly able—to dissect.

I sensed a general quiet emanating from the group.
Ah, I cried, if only I also could accede to doing nothing,
without it becoming a NothingDoing! Then, and only
then, would I have attained the ecstasy, the wisdom,
the whatever one might want to call it, a desirable
state of being: where no 'art' is produced, fashioned,
concocted, defined! And that, the being-there-in-abso-
lute-confidence, at the highest master level, that would
be quite the art itself—although that would be a meta-
phorical use of the term in this case.

That, I carried on with the assembled, is surely my nir-
vana, my desired destination. Or, is it?! I do wonder, tru-
ly, if the ultimate erasure of the NoDo, if going beyond
the NoDo, if the practice of the NoDo, should indeed

lead to the art of doing nothing. Or... Or... And I shudder when I say this: is the last of the NoDos, is the last of the NoDos, the actual art of doing nothing, in which case capital letters must appear: and the NoDo, the last NoDo, the ultimate NoDo is a 'neo' Art of Doing Nothing. Or, more precisely, the new Doing Nothing as Art: The nDNA? And thus, the NothingDoing/nDNA...

I dare not act, dare not say, I dare not—frankly—claim to know: for, the art of doing nothing might be the logical conclusion, when all the NoDos and, in essence, all other produced and created artwork, have been exhausted, and nothing is left—no artwork at all... Or it could be that the NoDo/nDNA—a mental and emotional space that one can attain, in multiple manners—is really just a damn great NoDo in its own right... Where to, where to from here...

·

From the NoDo to the nDNA—with the nDNA part of the NoDo family, and forever the two shall be attached and fused... Perhaps the NothingDoing/nDNA is precisely the point at which a clarity begins to emerge, a liminal state, an uncertain zone, but a hopeful zone, where the NothingDoing/nDNA actually precipitates, or prompts, or makes easier, the passage to the highest form of consciousness and engagement, the very essence and meaning of life: that is, the art of doing nothing...

I paused and looked at the assembled around the room. This must remain so, in the realm of queries and uncertainties. Clarity and uncertainty go together, re-member, I reminded the pilgrims: lucidity breeds un-certainty. Drown now in the throes and glory of the art form known as a NothingDoing. For now, drown in the NothingDoings. And one day if the blissful universe of being a master at the art of doing nothing awaits you, then that too, you shall reach, without effort, certainly, for that will be the logical way to reach the new land. Embrace it all, embrace it all for now, the Nothing-Doings as a whole, the art of doing nothing, and the NoDo/nDNA. No shame in the overall embrace. Never a shame in an inclusive embrace. And with that I leave you, I thundered at last, with the entreaty to embrace them all, including your NoDo/nDNA!

•

17. HePs

(A Heteronymous and Pseudonymous Poetics)

At the last of the hours, and for the last of the speeches, I gathered again the disciples.

All of the NoDos previously cited have had the common component that we imagined them to derive—or not-derive, in effect, and I must insist, it is *not-derive*, not, 'not... derive'—from *the same author*. I paused, for dramatic effect, and carried on. For, it is only by acknowledging this author and the lack of a creation—or shall I say, the acceptance of the NoDo—that we can identify with the fact of the NothingDoing.

There is, I paused again and peered into the assembly, there is another form of NoDo—another subspecies—although I hesitate because this new species... This new species of NothingDoing radically shifts to the practice of pseudonymity and heteronymity. An extreme adoption of the tactic—*nom de plume*, *nom de guerre*, call it what you will—that displaces the *'site' of the NoDo from the creation (non-object, non-expe-rience etc.) to the creators*—many of whom, unknown (those real entities having recourse to pseudonymity and heteronymity), or non-existent (the actual names standing for the 'false' ones), are in fact progenitors of NothingDoings by virtue of being associated with a non-existent person. These types of Nothing/Doings rest on *the progenitor becoming invisible—unknown and unrecognized and unmanifest*: a cultivated state that actually then allows for the NoDo to become real—more, a necessary condition to make it happen. Pseudonymity or heteronymity are not the only ways of the becoming-invisible that creates the species of NoDo sub-dubbed the HePs. One could even be so famous in some other field, or some other form, that any public would be reticent to connect one to anything else, and thus the fashioning of the NoDo. Whereas the NoDos, the regular NoDos, are the art-works, unmanifest and unannounced, of defined per-sons, the NothingDoing/HePs derives its NoDo-ness from the fact of the pseudonymity or heteronymity adopted by the NoDoist. The question is then: must the work in this case be a NoDo itself, or can the ac-tual work of the NoDo/HePs be a regular type of art-work, such as a painting, an installation, a drawing, or even a different type of work, such as a new form or a new hybrid, but that, in essence, does not conform to the most important characteristics of a NothingDoing, being unannounced and unmanifest? In other words, since the site of this NoDo is the *creator*, who *is* conforming to the characteristics of the unmanifest and unannounced mantra, must the work also adhere to those principles?

•

The importance of this query must not be minimized, I told the assembled, and, quite frankly, will depend on the functions and reasons-for-being of resorting to pseudonymity or heteronymity. Let us list a select number of reasons, in the hope that such a list will aid in answering the important query. 1) First, it is, as the little ones always show, quite amusing to 'become' other—think of our masquerades, our Halloweens, our dressing up as someone else. There is no reason to go deep into the psychology or the ancient rituals of this need to resort to being other, but simply acknowledging its universal appeal. A need, perhaps, but certainly, a praxis. 2) Second, it allows us an escape from the tyranny of names and categories, from the behaviors and stereotypes associated with our given names and the impressions and perceptions associated with the categories under which we are placed. A veritable unchaining of sorts—a delivery from the chains of attachments. 3) Third, the resort to the HePs allows us to become agents of reception/circulation in the world—that is, by 'becoming' someone else, we allow ourselves to read, and become in, the world, differently. 4) Fourth, becoming someone else actually allows you to inhabit a space where you do something different: you relate to others and the world differently, and thus, a growth into a *new self* takes place. 5) Fifth, and this cannot be discounted, it allows one to shield oneself from persecution *and* from fear of persecution (two different things), and from potentially being discovered and operated upon in any number of ways: disappeared, tortured, killed, paraded or what have you. It is literally a way of hiding, of not being found—perhaps a most primitive reason, but a very real and significant reason. 6) The HePs also allows for a new dynamics of interaction with others, in any number of communicative environments and situations, in any number of platforms. As those of us who have now become acclimated to the world of avatars and online identities know, we are positioned to act and be differently in various worlds, the physical one as well. 7) The HePs allows us to attack and undermine prevailing systems of associations with a certain practice. Without being identified, there is a liberty in the critique, in the figurative and, at times, necessary literal attack upon systems of thought, institutions and other types of endeavors.

I paused here as I could sense the onset of a certain

type of fatigue among the assembled. I had carried on without actually answering the more important query. Still, I needed to finish my list and said as much. A couple more my friends, I said, and we will move to the most important question. I must say also that the HePs allow us to: 8) Deconstruct how many political ideologies are founded upon false notions of identity and extended associations; 9) Go beyond the crazy cult of fame and celebrity that our culture has cultivated. It allows us to combat it, to ridicule it, to unmask it, to allow us to move more freely *as oneself*, paradoxically enough, without the burden of the cultural impositions.

153

·

Thus and so, I carried on. I needed and wanted to unveil these for the gathered. Becoming aware of the function of the HePs poetics would allow us to answer our most important question: since the site of this NothingDoing was the *creator*, who *is* conforming to the characteristics of the unmanifest and unannounced mantra, must the work also adhere to the regular NothingDoing mantra, that is, for the NoDo to also be unmanifest and unannounced? Or, could it be that any type of work would/could be a NothingDoing within the HePs realm? This was a crucial question of course, one that could undermine the very nature of the NothingDoings as such. I argued to the assembled calmly that the fluidity generated by the adoption of pseudonymity or heteronymity, and the serenity it would invite, would actually allow *any* work to be produced—and yes, here, one can use words such as *produce, made, fabricated, done* etc.—because none of it would be associated with the known and legal and recognized name of the artist. Within the realm of operation engaged in by the creator using the pseudonym and heteronym, there was indeed the fashioning of a NothingDoing, the NothingDoing/HePs. The subtle difference was this: the adoption of the HePs itself needed to be quite subtle, unannounced, and although literally impossible, made to be unmanifest. Not a loud and boisterous adoption of pseudonymity or heteronymity, but such that it is never perceived, never known, never acknowledged, never, then, real, never, then, manifest. It thus followed, incredibly, miraculously, that any type of artwork could be brought to fruition within the NothingDoing/HePs, since the NothingDoing resided in another realm.

I paused again and let the suggestion seep in. There was a great silence, a profound and contemplative silence. I broke it with a sudden and frankly unexpected laughter. Imagine now combining the NothingDoing/HePs with another NoDo—with the actual engagement in another NoDo that does not reside in HePs. That, my friends, would be quite the achievement!

NoDo square, doubly unmanifest and unannounced! A masterpiece of a NoDo, if there ever was one! I could see the smiles, but on some faces I also detected puzzlement, a lack of conviction. The assembled stood silently. We waited collectively and soon enough, in a rush and a madcap fashion, an applause came rushing through that knew no equal. The pseudonymous and heteronymous poetics: elsewho making and doing, toward a NothingDoing/HePs. And the potential NoDo square in the combining of the HePs and any of the other NoDos. They were imagining it, conceiving it, as hard as it was. As impossible as it seemed. But impossible it was not. What it needed was years of practice. The grand NoDoist, perhaps, the grandest of them all, would be its best exemplar... Yes, they were seeing it, these assembled pilgrims. They were sensing it. They were, maybe even, aspiring to it. Paradoxically enough. But they knew, they also knew, that the path forward was in the practice of the NoDos. The practice of it all. The applause simmered down. The noise fell. The breathing came back to normal. There was a long path ahead.

·

18. Pârt

And for the last gathering, I stood on a stage and peered into the field where everyone was assembled. Invisible they seemed, so magical the setting and so grand the number of pilgrims. This was not like the gatherings of before. This was not the gathering I expected. This was beyond all I could have imagined. This was beyond all anyone associated with the NothingDoings could ever have imagined.

This NothingDoing, I thundered, is *different* my brethren! And I emphasize *different*! Different from what we have submitted above, different from all the other NothingDoings in fact and in spirit. An altogether different essence to it all, an altogether otherworldly feel, my friends. This NothingDoing consists in recognizing the *miracle* that each moment provides. And more, recognizing that being *part* of this constant *strangeness* IS the work: not minor or major, not other or estranged, but *part*. No artificial separation and also no artificial desire or need of uniting in some corny or debatable holistic way. A different regime of being part of the entire spectacle. This is what gets repeated: the outside engulfing us, me, the outward, including us, we, as *part* of this grand shebang. This NothingDoing, the NothingDoing/Pârt, rests on the cognition, and recognition, of our being part of the world, part of the work, part of the fabric of the grand venture—its logical extension... Where absolutely nothing is 'done' and in this universe, the grandest of NoDo is elaborated! The greatest of works, the most liberating, the most magnanimous, the most unattached and unhampered work in the history of humanity: the greatest of NoDos.

•

Did we not, I thundered again, did we not so many times have the illusion that we were onto something when we thought of our actions, our banal actions, our everyday actions, as a type of performance—something grand, something magnificent, something absolutely fabulous, only to realize that, well, not quite! We were not the only ones or the first ones! How oft I have had to repeat this: we were not the only ones! Many preceded, many contemporaneously were engaged in similar practices, many followed. And often, these brethren who were engaged in a similar aesthetic and works, were met with one or another kind of scorn. How dare any one of them pretend to be fashioning art, they were told, when they were, in effect, doing absolutely nothing!! The counters were not difficult. Indeed, the theoretical foundations of these types of actions being categorized as 'art' were not difficult to expose, and we became quite adept at making the arguments and winning those arguments. Elaborating upon them, or adapting them in the given hostile circumstance, itself became quite the habit. What never followed, however, was the logical extension—or perhaps, even, the illogical extension, the ultimate, final, *reversal*: I, in the world, as spectator, *part of the spectacle, part of the art.*

And I thundered still as the masses around in complete silence breathless listened to my proposal. Consider these my fellow pilgrims, consider the artwork of someone who has conceived of all that is going on *as* artwork without declaring it as such, consider the artwork that is going on while we remain unaware, consider our own artwork conceived as all the spectacle that is going on around us... And then recognize, in these considerations and the embrace of being thus enveloped, the world's spectacle, and the Nothing-Doing/Pârt: the actions of others, the movements, the dynamism, all recognized and branded *as* spectacle, and our circulation within it, our being in it, our action within it, *part* of the work. More extreme, yes, than the previous declarations of 'I walk and that's art!' More extreme, yes, than the actual reading of any of our actions classified as art. More liberating also, the most glorious, perhaps, of NoDos, I thundered as never before, for, now, the conceptualization does not even turn to us—towards us, but *outward*, to all that surrounds us: the NothingDoing/Pârt does not rest on the re-configuring, re-categorization of our own banal engagements, but in the quick apprehension of the flow and interaction of events *as spectacle*, that is, *a type of artwork*—and our being part of it, our embracing it as just further part of the spectacle.

A most generous artwork then, the NothingDoing/Pârt. One that bestows upon others such awesomeness that our being part is deemed a grand venture indeed, a great honor, lo, a most desirable outcome. One that allows us to lose ourselves in the throes of this grand magnanimous work, this world that surrounds us. A most liberating letting-go. A most outrageous, perhaps, most unexpected of relations with all that surrounds us, all that is around us, in us, with us. A grand embrace. A full, all-encompassing embrace. A grasping of the wondrous strangeness of being, of existing, of becoming. The grandest of the NothingDoings, this Pârt. The grandest of artworks, the NothingDoing/Pârt.

·

Appendix I

Towards the Construction of a Future NoDo U.
(as in, The NothingDoing University)

1.0

It goes without saying that many will seek to engage in NothingDoings and will ask how one goes about becoming a NoDoist.

1.1

It will be a challenge to set this up. What are the foundations of the course of study to become a NoDoist? Or, what is *foundational*? How does one best reach that stage? How does one go about it? Is it really like any other field? Is it a field? Has it now become a field?

1.2

What about the competencies? And the modes of assessment? And the instructional methods? And the faculty? Is there a faculty? Is there instruction? Or, are you born a NoDoist? Maybe have the genes? The predilections?

1.3

One must also remember that the NothingDoings can be attempted and learned—and thus, one could argue, where there is learning, there are methods of transferring the skills and the behaviors and the competencies necessary to bring about the best possible NoDoist out of everyone. Or, can it really be learned? Perhaps it's a different path: not NoDo U. but the NoDo monastery, the NoDo retreat, the NoDo something or other.

2.0

Certainly, I and the few NoDoists I know are often asked, 'How do I reach NoDohood, O sage of NoDology?' And I am oft left with little to say, although I'm happy to engage the future pilgrims.

2.1

Perhaps this happens over time, in impromptu manners, when one does *not* seek. Maybe it happens through text exchanges or over morning coffees, maybe through informal conversation. Perhaps the best way is to model it.

2.2

Perhaps one realizes, within NoDo U., that there is no NoDo U., that it's an impossibility.

2.3

2.3.1

But the typology is there for all to read.

2.3.2

And since it's there, the invitation goes out to others to create new NoDos, that is, new types of NoDos. Mine are complete, but it's not impossible that others could create new types of NoDos. Maybe.

2.3.3

And thus NoDo U. leads you towards a passage, a ritual passage that is, when, upon conversations and exchanges and a completely whacky type of praxis in which you must practice the arts of NoDo, you are left alone to fashion a new NoDo.

3.0

3.0.1

The passage is supervised by a NoDo Sage.

3.0.2

The passage is supervised by a NoDo Sage who by definition is unattached to anything, institutions included.

3.1

We know that the NoDo Sages carry around no rubrics for the judging of the progress on the path. They have internalized the rubric. There are no grades or check-lists or even evaluations, really. Conversations, prac-tice, passage.

3.2

No tests either. But we'll know when you have reached NoDohood. I'll know. Trust me. I'll know. And I'm cur-rently the only one who can bestow NoDohood on anyone.

4.0

But, look, there are all sorts of edicts and precepts that are important and that we could perhaps develop.

4.1

These precepts will be unfolding and always develop-ing and thus there is no end to them.

4.2

We can only put down some of the edicts because, again, by definition, one is not thinking of putting down precepts. So, when they are illuminated and we have time, we put them down.

4.3

Precepts, misperceptions and how to overcome them, wrong-headed moves, heresies of various kinds, all these will be touched on.

4.4

Here ends the preliminary First Thoughts for a Future NoDo U. (Once enough funds have been raised to erect the NoDo U., we will hire consultants to work out the details.)

•

Appendix II

The NothingDoing Constitution(ish)

Article I

One major misperception of the NothingDoings is that they constitute a call to doing nothing. Absolutely false. Another major mistake would be to mix the engagement of fashioning a NothingDoing with the art of doing nothing. We have clearly shown how this is not so in the texts above, but it must be reiterated, especially because it is often as a compliment that we receive comments along these lines. Again, a Nothing-Doing artwork is not even remotely equivalent to the art of doing nothing.

Now, one could indeed foresee a very advanced No-Doist getting to the almost-impossible-to-achieve state where he or she succeeds in *enjoying the art of doing nothing with a NothingDoing artwork*, in which case, both have *fused* in the most miraculous of ways—in ways, frankly, that could perhaps not even be conceived. That, though, might be the absolute last state of NoDoist bliss, a certain relationship to the world, the self and others that is frankly, again, hard to conceive. One could even conceive of yet another, perhaps even more advanced form, an almost impossible stage of NoDohood, which would combine not only the art of doing nothing with a NothingDoing artwork, but do it *through* a NoDo, most especially and specifically, the heteronym/pseudonym framework (Nodo/HePs), in which one actually has become multiple and 'other' and achieves the fusion previously cited. As I write this, though, I realize that perhaps there is yet another, the most sublime state: that in which the HePs, the fusion of the art of doing nothing and a NothingDoing artwork are all merged with and through other NoDos listed above, that is, through any number of NoDos listed above: the NothingDoing/Nudge, for example, or the NothingDoing/OIK, or, again, any combination.

This is all nice and good master, you might be saying, but you called this a *constitution* of sorts! What kind of constitution is this?! The questions really should be along the lines of how we can adhere to the tenets, how we should follow the document! What are the ways, what are the lessons? Well, I'd answer, just reading this, walking around and thinking about it and thinking it (yes, direct object): that is the praxis. One might even be able to approximate this in comparative terms with certain rituals and religions, from meditative practices or contemplative paths to those philosophies that preach or suggest detachments and withdrawals of various kinds. Perhaps, we say, and we acknowledge this, but frankly, it's also more—more and certainly different... And you must be able to differentiate and particularize. Read this book, that's maybe where it all begins and ends!

Article II

A NoDoist is a rejecter of accolades and prizes. By definition. In fact, some of the principles of the NothingDoings lead to the recognition that accolades and prizes and fame and all that only come with conventions, with named works, often manifest in some way. Below we articulate some ways in which we can *assure* the *absence* of prizes and recognition and so many other ways of sinking into the abyss of convention, way too often cultivated, valued and recognized in our current cultural landscape.

1 Create works based on the theory that one must be working in the realm of territories without names—doing things that by definition have no prizes, grants etc. because the categories do not yet exist.

2 Create works that are profound and what you consider 'really good' but that clearly have attributes that will not make them widely digestible or digested: ambiguous, different, difficult. Although this edict functions with any number of works, the reader can see how works that are unannounced and not manifest will easily fall into this type of endeavor.

3 Operate within a political sphere that is counter to prevailing.

4 Be an actual and real rebel and anarchist. Engage in subversive activities. Real ones, that is. (Yeah, I know, who's to judge, right? Well, I'll be the judge. I'll be the judge of the actual and the real.)

5 Refuse to participate in those arenas that confer status in the present and statues later in life: degrees, ranks, medals etc... To the point of purposeful disengagement when it's possible, and later, perhaps, an active attempt at the dismantling of all that does lead to status and statues. This includes not engaging in practices that bring the phenomenon called fame and attendant celebrity—whether the banal type or the extraordinary type, the deserved kind or

the superfluous kind. And whether deliberately or because it's just not part of one's temperament. Meaning, no PR, no cultivation of critics, no social media, no newsletter, no announcements... Crucial all of this, crucial of course.

6 Purposely run away from endeavors that establish your name, or lead others to bestow your name on something: territories, honors, awards, buildings, stamps, schools.

7 Create works across disciplines and in multiple arenas. Truly cultivate doing things outside norm. Theoretically—but also in unexpected ways. At the margins of all. Liminal. (A nice place to be, quite frankly, if you have the temperament for it.)

8 Cultivate and deepen and expand your works with pseudonymous and heteronymous universes: a nom de guerre, of course, on top of the nom de plume. And could even fashion a nom de peace, and a nom de nom. And other nom de (blank) as necessary...

9 Fashion a life philosophy that champions the aesthetics and politics of moving on, along with the desire to constantly morph into differ-

ent persons—whether functioning in a different language or changing one's public persona.

10 Actually participate in living situations that diffuse any cognition of one actually being involved in all of the above! In other words, like a spy, a master practitioner of dissimulation, a trickster, go about your everyday business as if naught is a-happenin' because you consider your patrie, your home—where you are able to survive only through your spy-like and chameleon-like participation not even declaring any of the above—this strange universe that you have built. That is your home. Yes! Thus, fabulously reframing the necessity to make a living... And thus, truly perceiving the seriousness, gravity and importance of spy-like-living-among-all as would a foreign operative, or an acrobat on a tight-rope above the streets.

Article III

Choose *this* life. And *now*. Although there are sympathies with certain other movements and modalities of behavior, and certainly a trend of seeking the opposite of fame, a certain detachment and the utilization of the heteronym/pseudonym poetics, NoDohood does go beyond recognized forms of ritualistic belonging to one clan or another. It is a choice for *this* life: the acknowledgment that this life indeed has been chosen—even if accidentally—because of temperament, belief system, theoretical leanings.

The NoDo is bliss. It is the affirmation, as a piece, of this manner of being, circulating, existing as one and many, singular and multiple, present and absent, participating and not, among and not—and how all engagements, all manners of being, constitute in fact such a piece. Vanishing extolled. Disappearing, admired. Becoming-other, nourished. The mask and I... No, I is not another, I is others—and they, I. The NoDo is presence in absence, vanishing as appearance... The celebration of vanishing-as-appearance—and the smile that appears, the deep satisfaction, at the granting of this mantle, this prize, of liberty.

The NoDo is emancipatory. Emancipation. From all the names. All the makings. All the creating. All the seeking. All the wanting. All the belonging. Emancipation from the works and the œuvre. From presence and absence, after all. From itself even. And certainly from doing. Of course, from doing. That is the great call. The call from up above the mountain. The cry from the distance. The emancipatory call. O NoDo, O NoDo, O O NoDo, we shall not stand or pray or kneel or even bow our heads to you no—just acknowledge and move on.

Move on. And then not: emancipation from that even, from moving on. Stillness, silence. And then, from that too, emancipation. That is the great article of the constitution of the NoDos. That is the last article. The last line. The last word. That, O great NoDo, that is the last call, the last word. And not. That, O NoDo!

·

Appendix III

Minor Mappings

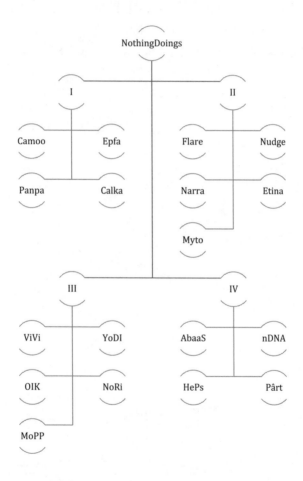

The NothingDoing Tree

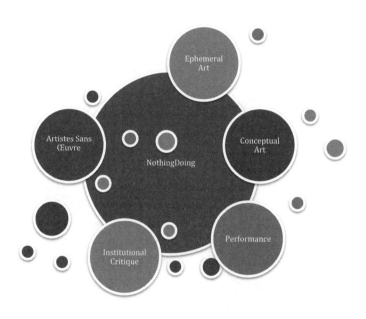

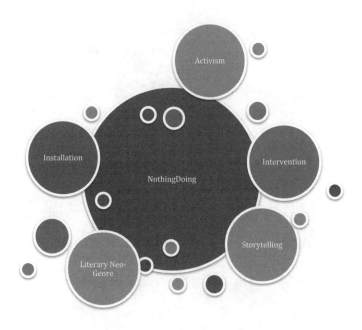

The NothingDoing Intersectional Constellations

Appendix IV

Page in Tribute of NoDo Dignitaries

A few examples of NoDo-like affinities. (Honorary NoDoists for the NoDo non-parliament?) There are plenty more but here we offer just a bite-sized sampling—a few morsels.

1. *Walt Whitman and his ideas on loafing. (Loafing must not be mixed with laziness!) More on this in upcoming Loafapalooza.*

2. *Image texted by apprentice from Nashville, Tennessee, October 24, 2013.*
Personal Note from Johnny Cash: "Musician Johnny Cash wrote this informal credo in the mid-1990s. Today the note hangs in his daughter Rosanne's New York apartment. 'I must remember that my 'internal Prime Time' is early morning and very late at night. This is when I think best—when I should write. Sometimes it is very important that I just sit around and do nothing. Rest every midday.' "

3. *The Judicious Doing of Nothing. Certain precepts from both religion and philosophy. Should be easy enough to read up on with a Google search.*

Okay everyone. And from here on out, I invite all devotees or potential participants or emerging NoDoists to send in their examples, or better yet, to almost send in their examples. Get excited, find other threads that are very close to the heart of the NoDos, think about sending in, but then refrain from sending... We trust you. You'll do it. And we'll all be happy in the end.

AFTERWORD

After Words

A series of lengthy explanations, non sequiturs, theoretical proclamations, digressions and drifts, Amir Parsa's *The Complete NothingDoings* often reads as a long and breathless cry, an atonal incantation of sorts; at other times, it becomes punctuated by imaginary dialogues and by the voices and silences of his interlocutors. Parsa inhabits his private Babel—or, as he called it in his *Tractatuüs Philosphiká-Poeticüus,* Baabol—and in an extended exercise of heteroglossia, speaks in many voices to write a hybrid book of speeches that is modulated by waves of boredom and entertainment, tedium and bliss.

The Complete NothingDoings is a manifesto pretending to be a systemic exploration of the practice of the NothingDoings (NoDos) governed by a deeply idiosyncratic logic as well as a life-style manual whose flowing poetics continuously counteracts any pretense of prescription and practical advice. It is a text that moves across a waste field of linguistic articulations adopting the visionary poetics of avant-garde manifestoes, the oratory of scriptures, and the rhetoric of business, organization, and managerial consciousness. *The NothingDoings* is between literary genres and modes of annunciations, and like many of Parsa's texts, it embraces, even cultivates, its own failure to expose and elaborate on its subject.

Echoing the manifesto culture of Western modernity and of the avant-gardes, *The Complete NothingDoings* calls to mind the Communist Manifesto, the declarations of Dada, the literature of Surrealism, the Situationist writings of Guy Debord and Raoul Vaneigem, and the texts of conceptual artists such as Sol Lewitt and Lawrence Weiner, while also resonating with Platonic dialogues as well as with other texts of spiritual enlightenment like *The Bible*, *The Buddhavacana*, and Nietzsche's *Zarathustra*. Parsa's prophetic tone, his first person address, his frequent usage of phrases such as "my brethren", and the overabundance of exclamation points bring into motion an array of textual references to confessions of faith and pronouncements of truths.

Moving freely, in a constant back and forth between wisdom and delirious nonsense, Parsa's manifesto-cum-manual, or as its subtitle states, "wondrous libera-

tion epistemopoetology" is prompted, quite appropri-
ately, by an instance of banal enlightenment, a blissful
incident experienced by the author while floating in the
blue-green waters of the Caribbean. Parsa's aimless
float, a feeling of both losing and being fully and wholly
in one's body, is paralleled by the structure of his text.
The prose of *The Complete NothingDoings* is like a
drift, a continuous flow of sentences and open-ended
passages about making and living life.

Parsa's text is both teachings and their satire, a creed
and its parody, and a rambling that defies any systems,
yet constructs itself as one. His love for taxonomies,
maps, charts and for systemic rendering of ideas is
a travesty of late capitalist self-help books, scientific
treaties, learning manuals and all sorts of educational
and organizational tools that advise their readers to
lead a life that is different from their own.

Written by a self-professed farceur, *The Complete
NothingDoings* is a play on the idea of a new life or
on "a new conjugation of being" (50), but it is also a
play that could, and maybe should be taken serious-
ly. The book's only partially hidden stakes are grave
enough. Parsa asks and answers questions that tend
to be avoided in a world where deeds are measured
according to their efficiency and usefulness. Is there
a way to frame an instance of bliss as non-commod-

ified experience? Can we argue for the sensation of floating in the blue-green waters of the Caribbean as something more than indulgence and indolence? Can living one's life without output, performing without producing, be activated into something rarified and exceptional? Can we live and continuously reinvent life by turning it into a Duchampian readymade?

And while we float in waters of any kind, how can we account for moments when nothing seems to happen? How can we account for just feeling and being? How can we be accountable for doing nothing other than just experiencing plenitude? Is it possible that sensations and perceptions—the non-quantifiable experiences that resist even linguistic articulation, let alone the imposition of productivity that governs our lives—can be traceless works of art?

The Complete NothingDoings is not a modest proposal: it suggests that neither objects nor experiences need to be produced and made, and it argues for a radical deskilling and the ultimate dematerialization of art. The book is about the refusal to make art by practicing any kind of ability or competence and by producing any new material or object. It is an invitation for the perpetual rethinking of things, whether texts or objects, and a call for the endless repositioning of perceptions, behaviors and experiences.

The NothingDoings are a systematic expansion and, at the same time, an undoing of all and every post-Duchampian paradigm of conceptual, post-conceptual and relational art. Parsa constructs a nebulous system where the various forms and subtypes of NoDos are charted and mapped as separate entities, yet on closer inspection they appear to be in volatile overlaps that destabilize their proposed taxonomy. Located at the intersection of method and madness, the capricious order of NothingDoings includes subtypes and species such as, among others, ViVi (the Viewer on View), Panpa (the Political Act of Non-Participation in Action), Etina (the Eternal Incomplete), MoPP (Moving Past Projects), and HePs (the Heteronymous and Pseudonymous Poetics). The various species turn out to be nothing other than the different aspects of the same thing—a profound repudiation of artistic authority, expertise and power.

Parsa's book is about the refusal of writing, making, creating and procreating. While it advocates for works without traces and a practice whose "most important characteristics" are "being unannounced and unmanifest" (151), it cannot seem to avoid its fate to become a book, a sole "document of tracelessness." (32) Is *The Complete NothingDoings* a pure and simple justification of Mallarmé's statement that "everything in the world exists in order to end up as a book?" Is it a record of the author's lack of discipline to resist writing and speaking? Is it a proof of failure? Not of failing to articulate and speak of, but of failing to remain silent?

Is writing a book about the NoDos a contradiction in terms, or is it an acknowledgment of those conditions which, since the rise of book culture, govern how ideas are disseminated and knowledge is produced? Is it an admission that nothing occurs until it has been branded? Cf. " 'I dare say, perhaps it has already occurred,' he says, 'and many a time!' With that, I disagreed. It has not, I insisted, for it has not been branded thus." (119)

If nothing can occur until it is branded, and nothing can be proposed without being announced and communicated, how can we be without doing anything, not even playing chess as Parsa's disavowed father and the book's specter, Marcel Duchamp did?

As one of the book's Venn diagrams—a residual trace of the demonstration tool in mathematics and in the managerial apparatus of postwar capitalism—tells us, the NoDos are situated on the edge and in slight overlap with the activities of "artistes sans œuvre" and a "performance." Since there are, of course, no "artistes sans œuvres" and everything we do is a continuous performance, the NoDos occupy a domain in-between impossibility and banality.

Amir Parsa

The Complete NothingDoings is an anti-art and pro-life manifesto—it is a call for floating in the Caribbean and playing chess—but it is also an activation and praise of indolence. Parsa turns the most endearing anti-heroes of Western literature, Ivan Goncharov's Oblomov and Italo Svevo's Zeno, into model artists and champions by redeeming their resistance to doing as art. He makes the "little corner of sloth" that Barthes wrote about in *A Lover's Discourse* into a capacious place, a site where one can be at home and reimagine life in a newly found liberty of laziness and inefficiency.

The practice of the NothingDoing is an endless deferral, a celebration of the unfinished, the abandoned, and the incomplete, and it is both an homage to and a tongue-in cheek parricide of the greatest indolent. "Affectionately yours, Marcel."

The Complete NothingDoings asks us to become the rebel sloths of a society that is geared toward endlessly increasing demands of creation and production. It begs us to recognize and overcome our learned helplessness, the lack of agency in "the incoherence, the chaos, the madness" (126) and "the flow and interaction of events *as spectacle*." (159) And indeed, since we cannot do anything about most things, why not do a NothingDoing instead?

The NothingDoings play on the efficiency, the use and the value of any and all kind of creative enterprise, and are at the crux of any possible resistance to the urgencies and impositions that order our lives in global capitalism. As Parsa puts it, they constitute "a *type of artwork*" which is "contesting the space and contesting the capitalistic and commercial thrust in everything (...) a glorious and salvific realm." (132) The NothingDoings are devices and tools to defer productivity, to sabotage the post-Fordist economy, and to liberate us from the task of making. They are emancipatory tools that free even their author from the constraints of meaning-making that is associated with the writing of a book. *The Complete NothingDoings* is about how to avoid doing art and embrace the art of living. "Yes, first, life." (34)

Can being alive be the œuvre we accomplish? And what exactly do we accomplish without leaving a trace? *The Complete NothingDoings* seems to suggest that the sole accomplishment we can aim for is to acknowledge the futility of doing and to accept our own mortality. Parsa's book appears to be about life, but like most things in life, it is ultimately about death— not merely about the death of doing, the degree zero of making, but about death *tout court*. As luck would have it, "it's always the others who die."

— Ágnes Berecz

Table of Contents

Bibliography

Tractatüus Philosophiká-Poeticüus
(2000, Editions Caractères; 2015, UpSet Press,
new and revised edition, with an afterword by
Gregg Horowitz)

Kobolierrot
(2000, Editions Caractères)

Feu l'encre/Fable
(2000, Editions Caractères)

L'opéra minora
(2000, Editions Caractères, limited edition)

Onomadopean
(2000, Editions Caractères; With H. Dabashi)

La révolution n'a pas encore eu lieu
(2003, Editions Caractères)

Skizzi Ska
(2005, The Elastic Circus of the Revolution;
Alternative Literary Experiences and Adventures (ALEA),
single edition)

Dîvân
(2006, Editions Caractères)

Sil & anses
(2006, Editions Caractères)

Erre
(2006, Editions Caractères)

Drive-by Cannibalism in the Baroque Tradition
(2006, Non Serviam Press; 2015, UpSet Press,
new and revised edition)

Ifs & Co.
(2007, The Elastic Circus of the Revolution;
ALEA, single edition)

And They Were Writing Their History
(2007, Editions Caractères; Translation of Bruno
Durocher's *Et l'homme blanc écrivait son histoire*)

Meet Me
(2009, The Museum of Modern Art; With
F. Rosenberg, L. Humble, C. McGee)

Fragment du cirque élastique de la révolution
(2010, Editions Caractères)

The Blond Texts & The Age of Embers

(2012, UpSet Press; Translation of Nadia Tuéni's
Les textes blonds and *L'Age d'écume*)

Le Chaise (Yes, Le)

(2016 and 2018, The Elastic Circus of the Revolution; Clan-
die, limited distribution)

Museo Equis

(2016, Museum Futures; museumfutures.org + limited rizo-
graphic edition)

Rev.Up

¡ôwhatarevolution!
Volume I
(2017, The Elastic Circus of the Revolution)

RiDE: On

(2017, Pratt Institute; Catalogue of the Risk/Dare/
Experiment series created and curated by Amir Parsa)

Onward with that Spunkedlic Avant-garde
Museographic Practices Œmnibus

(Contemporary Museum Education & Beyond)
(2018, Kadenze.com; MOOC with accompanying lectures,
texts, resources and participative contributions)

byk.rydlldor.set

(2018, The Felt; thefelt.org/issues/4/amir-parsa.html; eScroll)

Nel Mezz

(2019, The Elastic Circus of the Revolution)

Conceptual Conceptualism

(2019, The Elastic Circus of the Revolution)

ÉPÏKÂNÕVÀ (The New Definitely Post/Transnational and Mostly Portable Open Epic)

(2007-present, The Elastic Circus of the Revolution and other entities and organizations; plurilingual, multimedial and multiplatformal literary epic)

·

About Amir Parsa

Born in Tehran, Amir Parsa attended French international schools in Iran and the U.S., studied at Princeton and Columbia, currently lives in New York, and teaches and directs trans/neodisciplinary initiatives at Pratt Institute.

An internationally acclaimed writer, poet, translator, newformist and cultural designer and curator, he is the author of more than twenty literary works, including *Kobolierrot*, *Feu L'encre/Fable*, *Erre*, and *L'opéra minora*, a 440-page multilingual book that is in the MoMA Library Artists' Books collection and in the Rare Books collection of the Bibliothèque Nationale de France.

An uncategorizable body of work, his literary œuvre—written directly in English, French, Farsi, Spanish and various hybrids—constitutes a radical polyphonic enterprise that puts into question national, cultural and aesthetic attachments while fashioning innovative genres, discursive endeavors and types of literary artifacts. Launched in 2016 with *Le Chaise (Yes, Le),* a newly fashioned species are the 'clandies', works characterized by their clandestine dissemination.

In 2015, two of his books were reissued by UpSet Press, *Tractatüus Philosophiká-Poeticüus* and *Drive-by Cannibalism in the Baroque Tradition*. That same year, he launched his 'Seasons of the Manifestoes Global Barnstorm', a multi-year lecture/performance venture with stops in various geographic locations and related to a number of disciplines and emerging fields. He was invited to deliver the annual Samuel H. Kress Lecture in Museum Education at The Frick Collection in June 2015, while 'The Multilingual Literature Manifesto' was delivered in an actual barn during his Marble House Project residency in Dorset, Vermont in August 2015. Other manifestoes relate to innovative museum practices (*Museo Equis*), radical artworks (the theoretical foundations of *Le Chaise (Yes, Le)* and of *The Complete NothingDoings*), adventurous and artistic pathmaking (*RiDE: On*, the catalogue of the first three years of the Risk/Dare/Experiment series that he created and curated at Pratt Institute), along with a new world literature and the new literary epic.

Parsa has instigated his unique encantations, readations and bassadigas, and conducted more traditional lectures, workshops and playshops on avant-garde poetics, literary/artistic innovation, critical education praxis and cultural design at museums and organizations across the world, including Norway, Mexico, France, Brazil, India and Spain. As a Lecturer and Educator at The Museum of Modern Art, he developed and directed programs, projects, and learning experiences for a wide range of audiences, including the community partnerships, Wider Angles, Double Exposures and the Singular Educational Experience (SEE) entitled 1913: That Year This Time—a multidisciplinary course that took place over twelve hours in MoMA's galleries and classrooms. He also conceptualized and created the PinG (Poets in the Galleries) program at the Queens Museum in 2007, the Rooftop Roars & Riverside Revolutions in uptown Manhattan, and the RiDE episodes at Pratt Institute in Brooklyn.

With colleagues, students, and friends, he has launched in recent years the Museum Innovators' Collective and the Translation Innovation Ensemble among other initiatives, while spearheading avant-garde actions and changes in both museums and higher education at various levels. He also directs and orchestrates his own trans/neo disciplinary and literary/artistic/performative troupe, The Elastic Circus of the Revolution.

He is currently at work on several series and suites, including *La Pentalogia del Delirio*, *The Micro-Epic Decalogy* and *¡ôwhatarevolution!* , a projected eleven-piece suite of works exploring, interrogating and analyzing political 'revolution' through various mediums, languages, strategies and discourses. Recently, he was the artist-in-residence at The Museum of Modern Art in Bologna in June 2015 and June 2016, where he worked with a group of participants on cantos of *ÉPÏKÂNÕVÀ*, his ongoing, polylingual literary epic.

Parsa's curatorial interjections, performances, conceptual pieces and subversions, along with photographic, participatory and exhibition-based projects have taken place in a host of galleries, public spaces and environments. Overall and through the years, his books, transgressive literary works, artistic fusions and neo-disciplinary interventions and disruptions have dazzled and bedeviled, enchanted and pissed off, drawn praise and scorn, and punctured many an emperor's balloons. He has also operated and engaged in various artistic, cultural and political theaters under a number of pseudonyms.

About Ágnes Berecz

Ágnes Berecz is an art historian who has taught courses at Christie's, the Pratt Institute, and the Museum of Modern Art in New York. She completed her Ph.D. at Panthéone–Sorbonne University in Paris. Her writings have appeared in Art Journal, Art in America, Artmargins and the Yale University Art Gallery Bulletin as well as in European and US exhibitions catalogues. Her latest book, *100 years 100 Artworks*, was published by Prestel in 2019.